"You must be willing to do the uncomfortable, embrace the impossible, and do the unimaginable to achieve the inconceivable." – *Dionne Robinson*

For information on special speaking appointments or other enquiries, contact:

WalkInFaith Books
P.O. Box 441
Berrien Springs, MI 49103
E-mail address: walkinfaithbooks@gmail.com
Website: http://www.walkinfaithbooks.com/
Voice: (269) 588-0082 or (888) 469-0652

Get more inspiration from Dionne Robinson in her devotional book: *Experiencing God in Everyday Ordinary Things,* where she explores topics like never give up, dare to dream, you matter to Him, someone is praying you through, the amazing God of simplicity, and you are good enough. You will be inspired to believe that you are of great value, regardless of how you are being treated by others.

Read an excerpt and get more motivational thoughts from Dionne's personal website at http://www.walkinfaithbooks.com/

You can also find her on Facebook at *From the Heart Inspirational Picture Quotes* and *like* her page to get full access to daily quotes to boost your day.

The Journey

True Stories of Miracles and Mysteries That Will Transform Your Life

Dionne Robinson

WalkInFaith Books

WalkInFaith Books

ISBN: 13: 9781494268558

ISBN: 10: 1494268558

Cover design: Dionne Robinson

Books are sold through Amazon.com, Amazon.co.uk, Barnesandnoble.com, Walkinfaithbooks.com, Createspace.com, and other booksellers.

Because of the dynamic nature of the Internet, any web addresses or links contained in this book may have changed since publication and may no longer be valid.

Printed in the United States of America

Contents

To Almighty God!

For my dear mother who went to sleep four days before my scheduled flight to see her, and just weeks before this book was published. Zoebel Wilson (Ms. Zoë), the woman who lives in me, the woman who molded me and gave me a solid foundation of inner strength. I will continue to honor her with the life God has called me to live.

I'd also like to dedicate this book to all orphans.
To those who are broken, abandoned and lonely.
And to those who wonder if there is someone who cares.

Preface

A small SUV, a four-by-eight U-Haul trailer, and four eager travelers. Destination? Unknown. Our journey's end would be revealed only after two days into our expedition.

It's a journey that's bound to fail, but for God's loving intervention.

This amazing book is filled with true stories of miracles and mysteries, trials and triumphs. It is power-packed. Beloved reader, as you read this life-changing book, it is my hope that your courage will be strengthened, your hope be ignited, and your passion be fueled with each gripping story told.

These are personal testimonies of inspiration that have changed my whole family's life. Hope they will transform yours, too.

Dionne Robinson

The Woman I Loved

A Feature Story

An intense emotion spread rapidly down my spine, one so strong its ubiquitous presence could not be ignored. The gentle fall of colorful autumn leaves created a subtle contrast in the surge of my deep-rooted emotions. But amidst nature's beguiling displays, something was terribly amiss in my inner core.

Roaming through my heart was a strange, deep desire to see my mother. It had been nine years since I last saw her. And, my family's modest funds could not accommodate the costly trip. Within days of this intense longing I received a text message from my brother Earle. Mom had a bad case of Otitis Externa (ear infection). My desire to see her intensified. I prayed to the Lord to open a door of opportunity for me to see my mother, as it would only be through His intervention that this trip could happen. You see, having decided to raise home-grown children made for a stringent budget, which also meant that one paycheck could not cover all our travel expenses.

Then a miracle happened. A dear friend offered to help me purchase airline tickets to visit my mother. "Go online, Dionne, and look at the cost of the tickets.... You never know what God will do. Go now, and tell me what you see ... and if you are able, spend at least one month with your mother," she said. I acted immediately. I found a direct flight to my island home, Jamaica. My heart leaped with great joy. I'd cried over and over to the Lord to open a way for me to visit my mother. He answered me. A long-desired dream had come true. Then the unthinkable happened.

The door of opportunity slammed shut—without warning. Joy turned into crushing disappointment; laughter to unabated tears; excitement to overwhelming sorrow. My mother was gone! The fateful day? Friday, October 11, 2013. Only four more days to holding her hands, hugging her, and sharing belly laughs. I lost the long-awaited opportunity. Within an instant, life no longer seemed meaningful. I wanted to die.

I'd had so many disappointments in my life that I questioned the purpose of my birth. The profoundly disappointing experience of not getting a chance to say goodbye to my dear mother, the thought of her not meeting her grandchildren ripped my heart into a thousand pieces. *Why is she gone so quickly, so suddenly?* I asked myself over and over again, hoping to get even the slightest clue to quench the fire raging within my heart.

According to medical reports, she had died from a massive heart attack. "How could this be?" I deliberated. She'd gone to the hospital for them to take a closer look at her ear infection. Since she was diabetic, the doctors wanted to make sure that the infection wasn't spreading in her inner ear to the base of her brain. She was brought home dead!

The morning of October 11 when the hospital called my siblings in to discuss Mother's health, my brothers and sisters responded promptly. Upon their arrival at the hospital, they learned the painful truth: Mother did not make it through the night. But where was her body? Her bed was vacant. "She was taken to the morgue," one of the workers averred. Consequently, my siblings were not allowed to see Mom to "bid her goodbye" before she was whisked away. Hoping to get some sort of solace, I sent a message electronically to a childhood friend who'd been one of the nurses on the ward that fateful night, but received no response. My mother's death is still a mystery that is yet to be solved. Never in my life had I been this heartbroken.

I could not picture life without the woman who had raised me without a father. I loved her. She loved me. And I just couldn't imagine being at her funeral, seeing her in a casket. Eventually, I warmed up to the idea and braced myself to attend the memorial. Flying to Jamaica on October 15, as planned initially, was no longer desired. I was too broken to make the trip on that day. And, especially, since my husband, Don, was not able to accompany us at that time, we decided to reschedule our flight, making it convenient for him to be with me and our children. I could not do it alone.

On the rainy morning of October 23 my family, all four of us, arrived at the O'Hare International airport, in Chicago, Illinois, for our trip—just at the burst of daybreak. We boarded our flight. All seemed well. The plane taxied away from the gate, preparing for takeoff. Then the aircraft came to a halt and an announcement was made. "We are experiencing a mechanical problem that should be fixed in just about five minutes," the pilot broadcasted. The plane rolled back to the gate, and we waited. And waited. Before long, all passengers were asked to deplane.

Immediately, we moved toward the customer service line, the longest I'd ever seen at an airport. Everyone, including my family, who had a connecting flight in Charlotte, North Carolina, was anxiously trying to get on the next available flight. Not one flight would be available for us, and my mom's memorial was at one o'clock in the afternoon, the next day. This mission seemed impossible! Feeling the stains of disappointment trickling down my vertebral column, I moved toward the big glass windows that enveloped the waiting area and gazed in the distance as different planes fired down the runway, each leaving without my family. With a sense of desperation, I looked the agent in the eye, and said, "Ma'am, I am on my way to my mother's funeral. I've missed her in life; please don't let me miss her in death."

She expressed her sympathies, and said, "Tell my supervisor what you've just told me?" Her supervisor responded with compassion. We overnighted at a hotel approximately five minutes from the airport—all sponsored by the airline. The next day we would leave on the earliest flight to Charlotte, North Carolina. "This is going to be interesting," I muttered frustratingly. Tiredness was slowly overtaking us, as we'd lost more than a night's worth of sleep. How we would travel on the day of the funeral and arrive before the service was all done, puzzled me. Don and I agonized with God, wanting to know if it was in His will for us to fly to Jamaica. You see, I'd missed seeing my mother by only four days, then missed my flight the day before her funeral. Something felt wrong. The feeling within was petrifying, odd. *Was there a message in the obstacles for us?* I wondered.

At the hotel Don, Timmy, Arielle and I prayed earnestly. We'd also shared our plight with our friend Kemmoree who was quite instrumental in providing strong encouragement for our fainting hearts. She prayed with us and urged us to go on the next available flight, trusting that God would work His purpose for His greater good in us through this experience. We had a strong impression: In spite of the apparent setbacks, we must fly to Jamaica, regardless of the outcome. With the slightest snag we knew our attending my mother's funeral would not be possible.

Early Thursday morning, at approximately five o'clock—once again—we headed for the airport in the crisp Chicago air. We boarded our flight, but there was a tiny problem, one that was big enough to get in the way. Our seats were at the very back—twice on both flights. *Why the very back, Lord?* I pondered. Being at the back of the aircraft meant we would have to wait for all passengers ahead of us to disembark, cutting into the limited time we had to get to the funeral—and time was running out. With a sigh and a feeling of helplessness, I took my place at the window seat to which I was assigned.

On the flight to Montego Bay, I reached for my bag that had been stowed under the seat in front of me to get ahold of the printed words of my mom's favorite song: "They Are Nailed to the Cross." I'd planned to sing that song at the funeral. You see, with everything that had been going on, I had very little time to get my vocal chords tuned. Singing softly, I gazed across the vast expanse of the sky as the wings of the aircraft ripped through huge bales of cotton-like clouds. My eyes welled up with warm tears. A woman who had been sitting next to me heard me singing and thought it was angelic. I thanked her for being kind and briefly mentioned that I'd been practicing for my mother's funeral, which would be at one o'clock—just a few hours away.

Upon our arrival in Montego Bay, Jamaica, that lady did something unusual. She'd been traveling with a group of friends who were strategically seated at various sections of the plane. "Let these people through," she called to her friends who, by now, were trying to retrieve their hand luggage from the overhead compartment. Miraculously, people were stepping aside, bracing against their seats to let us move ahead—even passengers who weren't a part of that group were kind enough to let us go by. It felt like the Red Sea opened ... and we were walking through.

But when we got to Customs, there was another hurdle. By now it was approximately twelve o' clock in the afternoon. The funeral service would be in one hour. I looked across the hall nervously at the ocean of people. I spotted a lady with a friendly face. "Excuse me, Ma'am, I am on my way to my mother's funeral, which will be starting in less than an hour. Is there a way that our process could be expedited?"

"I am sorry, but I can't help you. I do not work with Customs," she said, "but you can talk with that gentleman over there..." I quickly walked over to the well-dressed man and explained my family's dilemma.

"May I take a look at your I-94?" he asked kindly. Then he said, "Come with me." Within five minutes we were all done. Only one more hurdle to cross: We had to get to our hotel, check in ... and get dressed. This took longer than we'd anticipated.

Finally, we were on our way to the funeral, which would take us no more than forty-five minutes from the hotel, provided that we had good traffic. But traffic that day seemed more congested than I'd ever seen—bumper-to-bumper for most of the journey. Minutes turned into seconds, and our arrival time appeared to vanish with every puff of smoke that erupted from the car's muffler ahead of us. My inner panic switch flipped on, and the red light of fear overshadowed my peace. *Are we going to make it before it's all done?* I cried within.

When we eventually arrived at the funeral service, they'd already started—way earlier than was normal for the Caribbean island. The church's senior pastor, I later learned, started promptly as he had another appointment and had to leave early. He was scheduled to give the opening remarks. Nevertheless, God, in His mercy, allowed me and my family to be there for the remaining quarter of the service. And I had the opportunity to sing my mother's best-loved song. Although the viewing had passed, I still felt a sense of relief being surrounded by family and hoped to get a chance to see my mother's face at the second viewing—at the grave side.

I also felt comforted being in the presence of people who'd known me since I was a child. My heart overflowed with precious memories, mingled with the intensity of grief of the moment.

Suddenly, my thoughts were intercepted by a huge gulp. The inconceivable started happening. I was choking, struggling to take clear breaths. My throat felt locked. I was clueless about what was happening to me. I didn't feel too good. Water. I needed water. I looked to my left. No water. I glanced to my right. Yes, there was water—a half-filled bottle of water in a woman's lap! I reached. I fetched. I drank. After about three sips, I was able to breathe normally again. Interestingly, this "angel" was clad in a Red Cross vest, sitting in the section designated for family, although she wasn't family. This woman saved my life. Could God have placed her there for me? Obviously, she'd had her share from the bottle, leaving just enough—for me! I never saw that lady again since that day!

The mysteries surrounding the trip did not end there. One week later, at around twelve midnight, we returned to the United States. With quick steps we made our way to Baggage Claim. Then, something caught

Don's and my attention: Someone was loading on one of our suitcases onto a trolley. Had we not been there at the time we did, our suitcase would have been gone! But the Lord came through for us, one more time—supernaturally.

Similarly, in the ensuing pages of this book, you will see the hand of God leading my family through the mystery of mysteries in various aspects of our walk with Him. You will also be able to get acquainted with His mysterious ways of endorsing and providing for my family's incredible journey of faith, right from its inception.

My husband, Don, and I had served as missionaries in the Far East, studied and graduated together twice, worked for the same organization—but none can be compared to this venture. This journey has trumped them all!

1.

Early Beginnings

"I make known the end from the beginning, from ancient times, what is still to come. I say, 'My purpose will stand, and I will do all that I please'" (Isaiah 46:10, NIV).

"One's early beginnings aren't always a reliable determinant for future success."
—Dionne Robinson

Big Dreams, Joyful Reminiscences

The wind creates a gentle rustle among the leaves as the trees dance gracefully in the shadows of the warm summer sun. And the ocean that once appeared languid suddenly comes alive. Small waves turn into big surfs, each carrying hopes that are deeply submerged under its formidable surface—dreams that swell and drift beyond the shores of expectancy. Dreams. Everyone has dreams, hopes that create inner ripples. They are aspirations that move one beyond the shallow waters of his or her ordinary existence to endless possibilities.

For some, all roads lead to California—a place where dreams come alive. But for me and my family, it has been quite the opposite. God has bigger dreams for a different time, another place. He wants to enlarge our territories beyond the borders of our small California town. But where would God lead my family? Would He lead us to a place where dreams are likely to diminish than fulfill? How would this dream be accomplished? Evidence of this dream could be seen and felt several years ago on a beautiful college campus on the hill.

It feels like only yesterday that I walked the sacred grounds of Northern Caribbean University (NCU), nestled in the nature-infused surroundings of Mandeville, Jamaica. Feeling the crisp, cool air that glided between the towering palm trees like skillful fingers on a well-tuned pipe organ; seeing the radiant blooms of the poinsettias that provided shade for curious students sitting on the "seat of the scornful"—all triggered a surge of hope that blew away every hint of doubt and brought dreams that seemed so distant to my fingertips. I can close my eyes and take it all in, for this is the place I can *dare to dream*!

It's been thirteen years now and the student population has quadrupled. Northern Caribbean University is home for students from over thirty-five different countries, which has made the university one of the largest Seventh-day Adventist institutions in the world. What had started out as a small college, known to many as West Indies College, has burgeoned well beyond its competitive streak into a full-fledged university, a status that was obtained in 1999.

As a student at this prestigious institution of higher learning, it was every girl's (who was single) dream to graduate not just with a diploma, but with the bonus prize of a handsome chap. Back then, the religion department had seemed to have the most handsome young men who were well groomed, polished—and looked holy even. However, in my mind, I had vowed to stay away from the holy men, as I'd heard whispers that a pastor and his family tended to be scrutinized beyond fairness. I wanted a private life, a relaxed one. But this notion would soon fade behind the horizon of insignificance. I would be smitten by the charming qualities and brilliant mind of a student I'd come to know—and love.

The Way We Were

It was February 25, 1998. The lush, green grass under the pine trees provided a soft cushion, and the tiny birds whistled cheerful tunes as though they were welcoming us to their habitat. Don and I were both in our junior year and had gone to this nature-filled area on our university campus many times before. This time, however, we were not there to study for another exam, but to communicate with our Master Teacher.

As we (seriously) contemplated dating, there was one thing that always stood immovably before us—honoring God in our relationship. We fasted. We prayed. We sought counsel from spiritual parents and mentors ... and the answer came forcefully and unanimously—we belonged together. Our relationship was too important to be left to chance, and God showed us favor.

We both had been baptized at the tender age of eleven and twelve. Looking back, we are now able to see why God had anointed us in those malleable years: He had a big assignment, a complex one that would require SEAL-like training.

During those burgeoning days of college, we dedicated our life to God as partners in ministry and asked Him to make us a monument for Him, to bless us with all the gifts we would need to complete this vital task—a request God took seriously. How the Lord chose to respond was more than we had bargained for, answers our hearts were not ready to embrace fully. The intricacies of our divine journey will be discussed at great length in later chapters.

Don and I had done a few college classes together, sang on the university choir, did many duets at chapel services, and at evangelistic meetings where he'd done his internship as a religion major. We'd even participated in college athletics. Don was handsome, smart, popular, and very involved, but there was one thing that stood out above all his visible attributes that I really admired (and still do): his solid Christian principles that guided his life. He walked in integrity. He'd also held several offices on campus, including vice president for the student association (known as USM), and was still able to maintain an almost perfect grade point average (GPA). After completing an Associate of Science degree in business administration, Don enrolled in the four-year degree program, where he studied the Bachelor of Arts in religion.

I pursued a Bachelor of Science in counseling psychology and favored a more low-keyed campus life. I'd go to classes, to the library, to the cafeteria, and then back to my job as a resident advisor (RA) at Jamaica Hall (women's residence hall). Making good grades and maintaining a consistent prayer life were top of my list, so I'd shy away from getting too involved in campus life. You see, campus was always buzzing with activities—all competing for one's attention. I chose what I could handle and stayed focused. After all, making good grades was imperative, as the university president, Dr. Herbert Thompson, would caution: "Your grades follow you to your grave..." I took that warning seriously.

If I'd been asked even a year before meeting Don if I'd date a smart, popular college student, I'd say yes to smart, and a definite no to popular. But as the years rolled by and friendships developed, we began to discover how much we had in common—we were vegetarian, last born of eight, peer counselors ... and ministry oriented—just to name a few. Our interest in each other grew steadily. Realizing how much we had been growing to love each other, we knew we would spend the rest of our life together.

The love we felt for each other electrified our beings and pulled us together like a million bolts of high voltage. Being together for the rest of our life was one of our deepest desires—and God desired it for us as well. We got married—soon after our August graduation—on December 20, 2000. This milestone marked the beginning of the journey of a lifetime.

When Love Found Us

1. And it came to pass in those days, that a noteworthy college student was passing by a classroom and heard melodious singing ascending to the rooms above a certain chapel. And, lo, the Spirit came upon him and led him to the chamber filled with singing.
2. After that brief encounter, behold, a little bug appeared unto him and bit him. Then a strong voice from within declared, "Thou hast been bitten by a love bug and shalt not seek treatment for the wound, for you have found unto yourself a woman, chosen by the Lord. Her name is Dionne and she shall be the mother of your children."
3. And there were on the same campus colleagues abiding in the field of education, counseling, technology and religion ... keeping a close watch on the progress of the young couple's commitment. And their associates muttered to one another, "Let us now observe, and see this thing which is come to pass, which the Lord hath made known unto us."
4. When it was revealed unto their parents that Don and Dionne were betrothed, their parents' hearts were filled with great joy... and avowed, "Mine eyes have seen thy salvation!" News spread quickly to neighboring towns and communities and everyone marveled at the wonderful things which were spoken of the young couple.

5. And so it was, that, while they were there in the Land of Wood and Water, the days were accomplished that they should be married on the 20th day of the most festive month.
6. Many years passed and when they had fulfilled the years of preparation, a son was born unto them and they named him Timothy, whose name means, God's honor. And as the Lord wouldst have it, another child was born, whom they named Arielle, a lioness of God.
7. Even though they understood not the saying which He spake unto them, the young couple traveled for many days from the West to the Midwest, as the Lord commanded, to raise their offspring in the fear of the Most High God. And so it has been to this day.

(Inspired by the story of Mary & Joseph from the Holy Bible, King James Version).

Note: This was written in a light manner to bring across the weighty message of God's involvement in the selection of a suitable husband for me. This was not intended to take the Word of God lightly or to trivialize its powerful impact.

Unforgettable Letters of Love!

These are but a few of the mountain of letters Don and I had written to each other during our courtship ... and beyond. Today, all I can say is, when love meets love the inevitable happens—they get married!

11/06/1998
At home

My darling,

I will not go to bed tonight until I've penned these thoughts, for they are welling up inside—they give me sheer delight.

My love, my darling, my sweet smelling rose, you are more than all the treasures of this world. I feel loved by you, and I am in love with you. The thought of us being so happy together these days just overwhelms me with positive emotions. God has really been to us everything that I thought He was—and more. Like I've said in time past, we have the right tools, we've set the right principles, but by God's grace we must follow through.

Tonight as Patrick Smith gave the analogy of the monks I thought to myself: What if Dee is the messiah? And what if I am the messiah? Baby, we both are, for "we're the only Jesus some will ever see." Let's show them who Jesus really is.

Mi Querida
De: Don, tu hombre

Cafeteria
11:11 a.m.
03/01/1999

My sweetheart,

Just a note to say I really love you and care for you. And whatever it takes to make us happy, I am willing to do—with God's help. I want to cherish your treasured heart. Dear, there is so much I want to say, but this paper is not enough to contain it.

Sweetheart, you are a wonderful person who stands tall above the common men on this campus. Please allow me, Baby, as well as allow yourself to love and be loved the way God wants us to love each other.

I am looking forward to having a wonderful supper with my adorable friend this afternoon.

Later.

From your sensational, sentimental D'.

P.S. I will always be there for you, no matter what. Don't forget.

Just for Love:

01/23/1999

Dee,

If I had to choose a thousand times over, you could bet your life that I would make just one choice – that's you, Baby.

Forever yours,

Don

10:40 a.m.

03/13/2000

Hi Sweetheart,

Dear, you've been running up and down my mind. You must have been extremely tired. I am wondering if you will ever find the energy to do anything today. Anyway, not to worry, I will give you some rest. I'll let you take a love nap in the right chamber of my heart. I will shade you, my sweetheart, with the delicate curtains of my love.

Honey, you make my life complete. You make a difference in my life. Like Solomon, I want to let you know that your eyes are like doves', and your countenance is one that is pleasing to look upon.

Baby, you are like many precious stones put together on a silver tray: whether it be sapphire, chrysolite, diamond, or gem, you've topped them all. The time will come, my sweetheart, when the spiritual, the social, the physical, and the emotional will be fused, will be blended like a sweet goblet of lemonade. Our thirst will be quenched; we'll be satisfied. Then, we will say: We have felt God's glory!!!!

Your darling,

D'

10/06/1999

Mi Amor,

As sure as night follows day is the certainty of my love for and commitment to you.

This is the dawn of our experience together, which will soon burst into a glorious day. Hold on in faith.

Love,

Don

Undated
12:40 a.m.

Hi Babes,

Have you ever wondered what it would be like to have a garden without flowers? The still, blue sky without sunshine? Or the forest without the songs and sounds of birds? Just think for a while. Thanks to El Shadai, the One Who knows what real beauty and genuine love is in its crescendo. Yes, He knows that you represent the perfect specimen of manhood. Within the chambers of your heart there is love of higher plains. There is joy that cannot be restrained, and there is peace that will remain.

D', you are a special gift sent by God. Our friendship didn't happen by chance. This special love that we share was implanted within by God, and God alone.

Let this love be like a tender plant. May it be watered with care, warmth, kindness, respect, acceptance and, above all, by the sweet Holy Spirit.

Keep shining. You are the sunshine of my day.

L-et
O-ur
V-ows
E-cho into etyernity.

Y-es
O-ur love
U-nceasing will be

D'-early beloved

02/22/1998

If every gift were as dear as this one—Dee—I suppose I would have to build a showcase to keep them. I would also need to employ the security for us to protect my rare collection. Yet, I don't think I need to do that, for this gift, though so precious, so cherished, so highly esteemed is one I can show to the world without fear of a loss. A mystery, indeed. Oh, well! I suppose I'm blessed. What can I say?

Don

2.

Commissioned

"Again Jesus said, 'Peace be with you! As the Father has sent me, I am sending you" (John 20:21, NIV).

"The Lord himself goes before you and will be with you; He will never leave you nor forsake you. Do not be afraid; do not be discouraged" (Deuteronomy 31:8, NIV).

"What lies beyond the horizon we do not know, but the Son of Righteousness shines resplendently from the suspenseful edge of the vast expanse of the azure sky, penetrating our hearts with His warm rays of love and assurance. He shores up our faith and lets us know that what rests obscurely beyond the blue is conquerable—because our Creator is already there."
– *Dionne Robinson*

Call To Missions

The sights. The sounds. The smells. Fully intrigued. The idea of embracing a whole new world with the man of my dreams at my side had made an internal stew of consternation and fascination. Indeed, it was a whole new world in more ways than one, and we knew full well that we would not get there on a magic carpet. No, it wasn't a figment of our imagination. This time it was for real.

It had been only three weeks since Don and I had said "I do" when our call to be missionaries to Taiwan was confirmed. Excitement streamed down our spines, anticipation of another new adventure flooded our beings. Our heads? Well, too engaged to figure out how we'd handle all that lay hidden in the shadows of the unknown. And the names of the city where our plane would land? That's another story. Upon our arrival at the airport of our flight of origin, the travel agent asked us where we were going, and that was when we realized that the names were just too long, too complicated—too suspicious, even—to pronounce. The agent must have whispered a prayer for us and hoped we didn't end up somewhere in the Sahara. We were just too enthralled by the blissful presence of unspoiled marital love, one that we vowed would last—forever!

We boarded the second leg of our flight from the John F. Kennedy International Airport in New York City, with a brief stop in Anchorage, Alaska, and from then on, the plane was expected to slice the air until we arrived in Taipei, Taiwan. What an adventure! For more than sixteen hours I stayed awake, wondering what would happen if I fell asleep. I glanced to my left, and sure enough, Don was already in dreamland. Across the aisle, there were happy babies cooing delightfully, while others perched uncomfortably on their mothers' shoulders, wailing as though they hadn't eaten in days. Behind me I could hear a few bones cracking as older travelers stretched their weary muscles. Feeling exhausted, I leaned my head on the back of my seat and let my eyes wander lazily across the roof, as though sleep were hidden somewhere in the overhead compartment, waiting for me to beckon and embrace its scarce commodity.

Finally, I fell asleep. But not for long. Strange sounds crackled in my ears. For sure the plane was going down. I jumped up, frightened and frazzled. I swiped at my ears hard; I almost tore off my precious assets. Still in a stupor, I groggily scanned the plane. No one else seemed scared. It was then I realized that what had appeared to be the sound of rapid descent had turned out to be the static from my ear phones. For the rest of the flight, oh, well, culminated in a loop of mere eating, stretching, and taking restroom breaks. My eyes had gotten so red that I worried that the natives would think that I was some strange being who'd just landed from space. Luckily, my glasses saved the day, and we received a warm welcome—in a strange, new language! This was the beginning of a great journey, the start of a new thing.

We would spend three adventurous years in Taiwan, teaching English and Bible in the after-school programs that our church offered. There were students from elementary through college. They loved learning English. The eagerness to attend classes was admirable. Nothing prevented them—not even dangerous typhoons. For Bible classes, several retirees would attend, desiring to know about our strange God while trying to learn a new word or two during each session. It was somewhat interesting to have my Bible students stopping me in the middle of what I'd call a spiritually-charged moment—the moment when you feel like you're on the brink of a spiritual breakthrough, just to ask the meaning of a new word, and then waiting to have both word and meaning written down.

I'll never forget the questions that hit the core of my faith. "How do you know that your God is the true God? When we pray to Buddha ... he answers our prayers, so why should we believe in your God?" These questions we'd never been asked before. You see, both Don and I grew up in a very sheltered, conservative culture, where one could find a church within every mile or so. Now, here we are, in a foreign land, being challenged about our beliefs. There was one student, in particular, who'd disagree with anything and everything that the missionaries presented.

She'd use her highly intellectual reasoning to derail our concepts. These encounters helped us learn how to prepare well before classes—although one never knew how a Bible discussion would turn out. Above all, however, we learned to call upon God often, because we could only touch hearts and change lives through Him.

When we were not teaching, our students would take us around town. I learned to sit on a scooter that was driven fifty miles or more per hour, with both legs hanging side by side, as though I were sitting in a chair. Our students knew some of the best vegetarian restaurants and therapeutic spas in town. Intrigued by their buzzing night market (a type of flea market), Don and I gladly accepted invitations to this rich spot to see the culture at its ripest. Foods of every kind could be found: squids, frogs, chou tofu (stinky tofu), snakes—everything! None of which enticed our appetite. We were content with eating red corns on the cob or digging into a huo goa (hot-pot) with yummy veggies. Oh, what wonderful time we shared together with students and fellow missionaries!

Particularly, Don and I liked spending time with our students, because it was during these moments that they would ask personal questions about our lifestyle. "Why are you vegetarian?" or "Why do you worship God and not Buddha?" some would ask. Those were precious moments that we will always cherish. Sacred moments sharing the love of God!

They Changed US—Or Did They, Really?

Before becoming missionaries we thought that we would be the ones to teach and change the people in far-away lands, but, interestingly, both the Occidentals and Orientals impacted each other in deeply personal ways: We touched their lives and they touched ours. They changed us—and we will never be the same.

Our missionary stints culminated faster than we could keep track. Now, the time had come to say goodbye to all the people we'd come to know as friends—great friends. We'd learned so much. We'd learned to be Christians. As we packed our boxes and suitcases, our thoughts, too, competed for private storage.... Don and I talked about the impact the Taiwanese people and fellow missionaries had made on our lives. The way we saw God, His people from different lands, Christianity: nothing would remain in its original form, except our strong belief in the God of heaven. Adjusting to a culture that was vastly different from our own while seeking to share our faith in culture-friendly ways, I'd say, added richness and meaning to the word—mission! In the end we felt more Taiwanese than we were Jamaican, for Don and I had immersed ourselves in our new culture, which had made it all the more difficult to say goodbye.

Our Next Step

It had been clear, however that, the end of a stint is only a step into another. But what would be our next step? We prayed as we'd always done, being confident that the answer would come. As we sought the Lord for guidance we could hear an almost audible voice, as though it were traveling in high-frequency waves, calling: "Come, I've got more work for you to do."

Deep inside Don and I knew we wanted to do more for the Lord. We sensed that God was leading us toward an academic preparation, an avenue to the next divine assignment. So we did as the Lord impressed and applied to graduate schools in different parts of the world, including the United States, England ... and the Philippines. We'd thought initially that we would study in the Philippines, since it was Taiwan's neighbor, then return to Taiwan where we'd continue working as missionary teachers. But God had other ideas in mind. You see, not every good idea is God's idea.

Our good friend, Sheldon Bryan, whom we'd met at Northern Caribbean University, had recently moved to the United States to join his wife, Terry. Sheldon had also enrolled in a master's program at a Christian university in Riverside, California.

"Why don't you apply here," Sheldon said, "it's really nice and the tuition is affordable."

"OK, we'll take a look at the website ... and see what happens from there," we assured him. Our interest grew as we perused the university's website. It felt like this was the one. With this impression, we applied. A few weeks later we received word that Don and I had been accepted into the university's masters programs to which we had applied—Don, religion and I, education. The process flowed smoothly. We were excited. But there was a lingering concern, a formidable roadblock. How would we obtain student visas in Taiwan, a foreign country? What's more, neither of us had a U.S visa. And, it's usually one's country of jurisdiction that would grant us such travel documents.

Student Visas: The Divine Process

We prayed. We boarded the bus that would leave at one o'clock in the morning to Taipei, Taiwan's capital, hoping to be given U.S visas at the consulate. Result? Visas, not once, not twice—perhaps, thrice: denied!

"Lord, what are your plans for us? We don't understand," we cried. The shoulders of our heavenly Father had been our pillows: the place we rested, cried, listened—right close to His heart. Don and I wanted to make sure we were acting in God's will, as in His will is the safest place to be. The answer remained unchanged: academic preparation.

"But what should we do? They are not giving us visas in a foreign country. They've denied us several times," we deliberated.

But a voice came back quite strongly, and said: *Be still and know that I am God.*

"How can we stand still, Lord, when our flights are scheduled to leave in a matter of weeks?" The voice kept quiet. In the silence we thanked God for the many ways He'd come through for us in the past, how He'd kept us safe from the deadly outbreak of SARS (a lethal respiratory disease that broke loose while we were there), and for allowing a narrow escape from the attack of hundreds of angry bees that congregated above our front door in Kaohsiung. These experiences we counted as blessing in disguise, and claimed in faith that, God would come through for us again. We were confident of His promise: "Trust in the Lord with all your heart and lean not on your own understanding; in all your ways acknowledge Him, and he will make your paths straight" (Proverbs 3:5, 6). We knew God wanted us to trust Him, and we believed He'd come through—but how? When?

The Message That Changed Our Life

One sunny Kaohsiung day when the sky seemed so clear that I could write my thoughts on it, I wandered about the yard that was also home for our local church—just to breathe and to take in my surroundings. As Bible and English teachers instructing second-language learners, we'd soon come to realize that taking a breather was vital. The nearby streets hummed with scooters of all sizes, each one carrying at least a family of four—and a couple of Chihuahuas, too. Just a few blocks away the sound of laughter faded in the ocean of busy traffic. "A very busy day," I muttered.

In my own mind the traffic of my thoughts lined up, one behind the other, like a congested city street. Then like an impatient driver rushing ahead of a long line of traffic, a thought moved to the forefront of my mind, and transported me back to some of the great times Don and I had had. The bumpy ferry rides across choppy waters to Green Island (a small volcanic island, approximately twenty-one miles off the eastern coast of Taiwan). Not exempting the passengers who hacked and regurgitated, and the curious ones who nervously attempted to practice their English with two foreign missionaries. It was particularly exciting to ride scooters around this tiny island, in just about forty-five minutes, admiring the breath-taking landscapes and interesting rocks.

During our first summer break, some of our students had suggested that we visit Thailand to see the different of types of Buddha statues: some of these images were decked in gold and displayed meticulously in exquisite temples, where shoes were not allowed. Others were embedded in trees and walls. We'd even ridden on the backs of humongous elephants as they lumbered across low-traffic streets.

Our tour guide would not let us leave without having us ride in an old wooden canoe down a canal of swift, muddy currents to the famous floating market. There, we ate indigenous fruit. Durian (known in Asia as the "King of Fruits") and mangosteen were our favorites. Only a blocked epiglottis could stop us from eating those delicious fruit. As I relished the assortment of pleasant memories, a scooter zoomed by like an angry bee ... and jerked me from the confines of my own thoughts. Then I heard a voice. Someone had been calling.

"Dear?" *It's got to be me since no one else calls anyone dear around here, except my husband,* I thought. I turned around. I was right. It was Don calling out to me. He seemed to have an urgent message.

"Check the computer," he urged.

"Why?" I probed.

But he refused to reveal what he'd seen. My curiosity piqued as I sensed it was something important—very important. I hurried up the narrow staircase that led to our apartment on the third floor above Pastor Mark's apartment. My inquisitiveness mounted with every step. Panting and sweating, I hurried to the computer, which already had important information waiting for me. It read: "The U.S. Department of Homeland Security and the U.S. Department of State today suspended two programs that allow certain international air passengers to travel through the United States for transit purposes *without first obtaining a visa.* The programs, known as the Transit Without Visa program (TWOV) and the International-to-International transit program (ITI), have been suspended. The action takes effect at 11:00 a.m., Saturday August 2, 2003" (Homeland Security).

My eyes grew big. My jaws dropped open. I could hardly believe what I saw. *Lord, are you changing the rules of the United States to accommodate us? Could it be?* I wondered as a myriad of possibilities appeared on the database of my mind.

We prayed, and then quickly made an appointment to go back to the consulate in Taipei. Taipei was approximately a seven-hour trip by bus from where we'd lived in Kaohsiung. We'd have to take the bus at one o' clock in the morning and get some shut-eye on the journey—an almost impossible feat.

The Shaded Window

When we arrived at the embassy on that blessed July morning, we had butterflies in our chest. *Did we do the right thing in coming back so soon after so many denials?* What's more, we'd even been more nervous about going back to the same consular officer who had denied us visas weeks before.

Don and I stood in line. I looked at my fingers, and my nails had suddenly seemed like satisfying pacifiers. I needed to stay calm and rest in God's assuring promises: "Surely I am with you always, to the very end of the age" (Matthew 18:20), the voice in my head reminded me... *It'll be all right!* I told myself. Don and I breathed a sigh of relief when we noticed that we would be going to a consular officer whom we hadn't met before. What a relief. Then the unthinkable happened!

The "new" consular officer suddenly pulled the shade down at her window. *Lord, where is she going?* I worried, *please let her come back.* Several minutes passed and still she did not return. All the other lines to our left and to our right were moving quickly. We could hear the Taiwanese applicants saying xiè xiè (thanks) while smiling from ear-to-ear. *Lord, will you put smiles on Don's and my face, too?* I prayed. The answer was still uncertain. Then the shade at our window moved up slowly—almost like a suspenseful scene straight out of the movies—and who do you think was standing there? The very consular officer who'd interviewed us a few weeks before! The very one we had dreaded seeing again. Don looked at me. I looked at him ... then winked at each other to say *it will be all right.* We prayed silently. I looked at the window and realized that the consular officer was staring at us. It felt like a bad dream.

"Next," a voice called.

It was our turn to face the person whom we dreaded. *Lord, you are in control,* we breathed. What happened next still remains a mystery.

"How can I help you?" The consular officer asked in a flat voice as if to say *Look, you guys were here just a few weeks ago ... so why are you here so soon?*

Don spoke up. "We are taking your advice to go to Jamaica to get our student visas. Also, we've read the recent news on the adjustments made to transit visa regulations ... so we are here to apply for transit visas to go to our country of jurisdiction to get our student visas..."

The consular officer looked us directly in the eye. There was a brief pause, one that felt like we were hanging in space on a strand of thread. When he eventually spoke, his response was nothing short of a big surprise—his words caught us off guard!

"I am going to give you and your wife visas that will allow you both to visit your family and friends in the United States ... but you cannot study on it," he said.

Did I just hear what I think I heard? I was even afraid to ask too many questions or appear too happy, lest the officer changed his mind. So we acted as though we understood everything. The truth is, we didn't. But we left with smiles, just like the Taiwanese. The air around us felt a bit holy as we spent the whole time (when we got outside), praising and thanking God for making the impossible possible.

Within ten days, we had our passports in hand. We studied the pretty stamp carefully. We now had visas stamped in our passports! Expiration date? Ten years later!

"Foreigners don't get visas in Taiwan," some of our fellow missionary friends would say disbelievingly. We may have been just strangers in a foreign land, but to our heavenly King, we were ambassadors on a mission for Him. Without delay He sent a command that no human could ignore. God gave us not one-time transit visas that we had applied for; instead, He gave us ten-year visas, ones for which we did not apply! What a God! Our Lord had changed the law of a powerful land for two ordinary missionaries in a foreign country. Indeed, "nothing is impossible with God" (Luke 1:37).

Within a few weeks, Don and I would say Zài jiàn (goodbye) to some of the finest students we'd spent months and years interacting with. We flew to the beautiful Land of the Free, went to our homeland, Jamaica, where we'd apply for student visas. Result? Visas granted. God did it once again. We headed to the friendly campus of La Sierra University, where Don would pursue a master's degree in religion, with a school psychology emphasis, and I, a master's in curriculum and instruction, with specialization in teaching English as a foreign language.

3.

Remarkable Provisions

"And my God will meet all your needs according to his glorious riches in Christ Jesus" (Philippians 4:19, NIV).

"There is no way to express how great God is!"
— Arielle Robinson

An Unexpected Opening

Graduation was now on the horizon and obtaining appropriate jobs seemed as distant as the sun. We combed through newspaper classifieds, scoured Internet ads. Nothing. Then, one day a job emerged on our religious organization's website. A perfect job, but an unasked for location. There was no way we were going to put down roots at a place out in the middle of nowhere. We checked back with the website often for new listings, hoping we'd get a chance to stay in the Riverside area, not too far from La Sierra University. We had friends there, a very supportive environment. But, quite interestingly, that one job seemed to have Don's name written on it.

Out of sheer curiosity, Don submitted an application for the job while he explored other options. For days I flipped through mental images of my family living in this small town, getting lost, and even vanishing without a trace. How would we survive? What if we had children there? It was frightening. Then the phone call came! Don was contacted for an interview. It was really happening. Little did I know that the treasure I was seeking was actually hidden on the other side of my fears. Indeed, a chest of treasures was about to pop open—slowly, and, in time, we would discover glittering gems.

That morning when Don went in to be interviewed for the religion teacher position, we didn't know what to expect. What we were certain of as we prayed, however, was that our God was at work. The meeting came with an interesting twist. Somehow, during the interview, Don mentioned to the principal that I'd been a teacher, too. As the Lord would have it, there was an opening for me as well, unbeknown to us. The principal asked if she could meet with me that same day. Meeting with her was an opportunity I did not want to miss, but getting time away from my two part-time jobs—at two separate public schools—to attend the interview was daunting. I did not have sufficient time to speak with my supervisors. Nevertheless, I put in a last-minute request. I got the green light. Everything fell into place easily and quickly; it scared me a bit.

That afternoon I headed out to the conference office, where I would meet with the principal, Mrs. Smith, along with Mrs. Havens, one of the superintendents. Up to this point, I had no formal application on file for the job, but God did something praiseworthy. He gave me the job, anyhow. Now, the question that lingered was, should we accept these new job offers or keep on looking for something in the Riverside area? Were we prepared for the adventures ahead? Principal Smith invited us to go and see the school and the area. We went that same week. The welcome we received was totally unexpected, however.

A Torrid, Yet Fertile Desert

Upon our arrival at the school in Calexico, I opened the door of the car that we had traveled in for more than three hours, but had to close it immediately. Our welcome was not what we'd bargained for. We could hardly stand it. It was the hottest temperature we'd ever experienced. It felt like I was about to be tossed into a furnace. When I eventually emerged from the car, along with Don's parents, and aunt (who had come for our graduation ceremony), I could almost feel the hair on my skin singe—and it was only June! One worker smiled and said, "In August you will receive an even warmer welcome." And she was right. Despite the torrid temperature, in spite of the sweltering heat, we spent six years there—six fruitful years.

Generally, a desert is supposed to be barren based on its classifications and characteristics, but for us, though, the desert was everything but barren—it offered us an oasis. It was there in the desert that our children were born. It was there we bought our first five-bedroom house that we later gave up to make staying at home with God's treasured gifts, our children, possible. Some persons could not wrap their minds around our decision, but as for Don and me, it wasn't a difficult decision. We'd concluded that it's either we pay now or later. We chose now ... and embraced the challenges of temporary discomforts. For us, nothing in this world is more valuable than joining God in raising the innocent children He's given to us. To our children we will cling, for they, too, have been built for the mission. It was in the desert that we felt our greatest joys and sorrows. It was there, in the desert that, we experienced our burning-bush experience like Moses. And, it was there, in the desert, we started one of our most amazing journeys with God!

A Prayer, A Voice, And an Unforeseen Response

The time had come to start a new phase beyond the borders of the scorching desert. Although there were many wonderful people who'd been a part of our life for six years, we knew, indubitably, the time had come for us to say goodbye. It had been our prayer that God would lead us to a place close enough to my island home to make it easier for my mom to visit. We'd also prayed for a quiet country side to raise our two young children. Someplace where they could squeal delightfully as they run in the rain barefooted and taste the cool rain dripping down their foreheads.

As kids growing up in the country, Don and I enjoyed playing in big yards, running around safely on several acres of land, and picking all kinds of fruit that Mother Nature offered. There were dozens of children our age in our neighborhoods—and we desired a similar environment for our children as well. Looking back at those growing-up years of crazy fun had made each moment of my reminiscences wonderful.

We talked with God about our desires and asked Him to lead us to a beautiful countryside where our children would be able to interact with nature. We prayed for more than a year. Finally, we got the nod to move on. However, we were in for a big surprise! You see, when we pray we do not always understand the full spectrum of what our requests necessitate. This holds true for us, as we were about to discover that what we'd prayed for was much bigger than what we could comprehend. God was about to take us on a journey, one He would make sure we never forget!

With the full itinerary remaining a mystery, we knew, nonetheless, it was time to start packing. We started looking into renting a moving truck. But we had it all wrong. After telephoning the conference office (our employer) to make arrangements, things just seemed not to be coming together, so we asked God—again—what He had in mind for us. The answer that came back to us wasn't one we'd anticipated.

Do not take your belongings, a voice said.

We argued that what we'd heard couldn't be right, as we would need our furniture, appliances, and all the stuff we'd owned. Everything we possessed had suddenly seemed important and necessary. So, we continued to make plans for getting another moving truck from a different company.

Then the voice came back even more forcefully, as if to chide, "Leave all that stuff. I'll take care of you."

With a hint of reluctance, I listened. Don and I sensed, quite strongly that, we were no longer in charge and that the journey we were about to take was outside our control. For me, I always liked to have things all organized, knowing what was going to happen next and so forth, but this time, I knew I'd have to relinquish that part of me to Someone wiser. This time I'd have to be still ... and listen, because Someone outside of me, Someone more powerful was speaking, and I felt compelled to obey.

Do you mean that God actually cared about us ordinary, mistake-making human beings so much that He would take the time to respond almost audibly to our feeble petitions? Yes, He cared enough and He still does. And, He cares about every detail of your life, too. You don't have to be perfect. He wants you to be enthusiastic about following Him. God will meet you where you are and take you where you ought to be, if you are willing. I must confess that it did take some adjustment. It was not easy to decide what to take and what to leave behind.

Being in this sticky spot, I suddenly understood what Lot's wife must have felt when the command was issued to leave Sodom. It's not always easy to separate oneself from stuff and move forward with God, trusting Him to take care of our needs. Like Job, I learned to say, "The Lord gave me what I had, and the Lord has taken it away. Praise the name of the Lord" (Job 1:21). Sensing that the Lord was serious about what He'd said earlier, Don and I started a new phase of adjustment. Our thoughts shifted from renting a moving truck to securing a U-Haul trailer. The size? We'd better leave that alone until we received further guidelines. And the instructions did come, ones that made us stop in our tracks.

"Hon, I've rented the trailer," Don said happily.

"How big is it?" I asked curiously.

"A four-by-eight trailer," Don replied.

"A four-by-eight? That means we are really leaving our stuff." I muttered.

For the first time everything felt so real. I sat quietly for a long while contemplating a new future—without the stuff. It was then I realized that the journey God was about to take my family on was much bigger than I could ever understand. Without delay an intense purging began, not just physically, but emotionally and spiritually as well.

Unexpected Sales

One quiet Friday morning when the weather had decided to be kind, Jesus stopped by our home. Jesús Garcia, a good friend who had the character of His Lord, visited us. We told him we were getting rid of almost everything.... He stood pensively for a moment.

"Why don't you have a garage sale? Hispanics love to shop .... I believe you could get everything sold," he urged.

"Hmm, I think we are not at a great location; besides, we've never done this before," Don and I countered.

But a voice inside said, "Listen to him."

And we did. It was approaching midday and we thought it would be too late to start a garage sale. Nevertheless, we made a sign (a pitiful one) and put it on a pole near the main street. What happened next is nothing short of a miracle. While we were putting stuff out on the lawn, people were coming in—practically out of nowhere. What's more, they were not just looking, but buying! Excitement began building and we took out more items ... and those went quickly, too. One neighbor across the street whom we hadn't met before came by our home out of sheer of curiosity. He said, "I noticed you put just a few things on the lawn, but I kept seeing people going into your house and leaving with stuff ... I'd like to buy something too."

Then, there were two customers who wanted a kid's bike we had up for sale. As the gentleman passed and saw the bike, he motioned to us that he was interested. But before he could park his truck to get across the street, someone else came and fetched the bike. And, of course, he wasn't happy that he'd missed the bicycle. To appease him, we gave him a toy for his little kid. Not sure if that helped, but he did seem all right after that.

By early evening, long before sunset, almost everything was sold! We'd lived in that community for six years and had never met half of the people we encountered that day. It was like our home had suddenly become their home. Every day leading up to our departure, we would meet someone new, someone who wanted to purchase something. And the ones who could not afford to buy, we gave them the stuff, anyway. The relationships formed and love shared over those few days could have only happened through an unseen hand.

These memories warm our hearts each time we reminisce. It was more than just a simple garage sale; it was a spiritual encounter, an enriching experience. It created an opening for witnessing that we hadn't thought of. We had a chance to pray for persons who shared and opened up their hearts ... and as they leave, we gave them small inspirational books and tracts. This was and still is an unforgettable experience, and God chose the last few days to show us what He was capable of doing, so we could begin to trust Him more for the journey ahead.

The Last Meal

The house was now empty, but filled with the presence of God. The atmosphere felt light, which triggered a strange feeling of liberation. Surrounded by open spaces that furniture and appliances once filled, we looked at each other, and then sat on boxes to eat our final meal before the journey. A large blue container became our table, and buckets, our stools. We ate a happy meal without missing the things that were gone. Only the walls stayed, bidding us continuous goodbyes.

Friends from our community and our church came by to help us with our final packing, but there was a problem. We had to unpack the U-Haul trailer, as it could not hold everything we wanted to take. Then, the voice came back and haunted us throughout the night as we retired on a makeshift bed on the floor. I looked to my right, and the kids lay sound asleep. For them, it was almost like nothing was different. But for Don and me, nothing was the same, except our love that remained unshakable. As the kids slept, my husband and I wrestled with the Lord in prayer. We felt that the Lord wanted us to get rid of more stuff.

Earlier in the day, we'd thought about renting a bigger trailer, but the voice came back, quite strongly—as if to reprimand us—and said: *No. Get rid of more stuff.*

"What should we do?" we asked each other, as we thought we'd kept back everything we assumed was important. "Did we not obey?"

Nevertheless, we went back into the trailer the next morning, unloaded the boxes and suitcases and got rid of more things. Some kind neighbors and friends from our church—Mar, Liza, Jesus, Susanna, Lorena, Roger and Judy offered much-needed help. Roger and Judy brought us sumptuous blueberry muffins for breakfast, along with games the kids could play during the road trip. Lorena offered us subway sandwiches and cute paraphernalia for the journey as well. Mar, Liza, Jesús and Susanna helped us with getting our belongings organized. We felt cared for.

Unpacking and repacking had caused us to leave a day later than we had planned, but it didn't matter because we felt God's peace and knew He was with us. God's presence had been even more evident when we remembered how He had provided money for the journey—miraculously!

An Unanticipated Gift

With uncertainties lurking in the shadows, my family realized that this cross-country move would require much faith. There had been a time when we would pray for God's revelation (in regards to where He'd like us to relocate), and would hear echoes of silence only. Every day we'd pray and watch to see how God would answer, but no word we would receive. Wanting to stay in God's will and to make sure that the move was God-approved, we asked our new pastor and mentor, Pastor Julio Tabuenca, to join us in prayer.

We'd only met Pastor Tabuenca a few months before my family's relocation plans intensified. He was the kind of person that anyone would want to sit and talk with. He was so connected, so intentional about knowing and doing the will of God. Pastor Tabuenca made serving God a delightful experience. He'd brought so much life and hope to our small church—to the whole Imperial Valley, in fact. He'd come to our small church after our senior pastor had left suddenly. This, in itself, was divine intervention. As soon as our new minister took on his role as interim pastor, he met with the elders where we discussed and prayed about the possibility of having a seminar called "Experiencing God." This seminar would later provide food for our faith and fuel for our hope as we prayed and prepared to move. Don and I never foresaw having our own burning-bush experience in the desert, until we participated in the "Experiencing God" seminar. We felt connected with God in a way we had never experienced before. One day while preparing for the seminar, I felt impressed to contact Pastor Tabuenca.

"Pastor, we've been praying for God to reveal to us where He would like us to go specifically, but still haven't received an answer," I shared over the phone, "what should we do?"

"Well, let's see. I will join you and Don in prayer for seven days. At the end of the seven days, we will share what the Lord has revealed," Pastor Tabuenca assured.

"OK, Pastor, we'll do that," I responded, feeling somewhat relieved.

Day one, day two ... day six past and we still did not hear word from the Lord—clearly. Don and I kept our eyes and ears opened to every cue that could crack this spiritual puzzle. Every evening when Don got home from work, I'd ask or he would ask: "What did the Lord say to you today?" That question would begin to define the new phase we were about to undertake. Doubt crept in at times, however, and we wondered if (by the slightest chance) the Lord had wanted us to stay in California. Then the seventh day came. We still had no special word from above. What did the Lord reveal to our beloved Pastor T? We were eager to find out! By now Pastor Tabuenca had started his trip to meet Don at his classroom at the Mission School. (Don had been a Religion and Math teacher there). I would join them from home via webcam.

As our beloved Pastor arrived at Don's classroom, the kids and I huddled around the computer and waited eagerly. We had been looking out for something dramatic, not necessarily a voice calling from the heavens, but for something that would give a clear, unmistaken direction. So as we met, we thought nothing special or specific or new had been impressed in those seven days of prayer. But the Lord had other plans. In fact, great plans for this willing family.

During this spiritually-charged moment—via webcam—I sat spellbound. Don and I didn't have much to share since we did not receive a special message during the seven days of prayer. When it was Pastor Tabuenca's turn to speak, he broke the silence—powerfully. He spoke deliberately. What he revealed that afternoon would be forever etched in our hearts.

"It was brought to my attention that you'd need money for your journey. Someone has given you one thousand dollars ... that will be made available to you [in a few weeks]. This is for you and your family to travel together on this journey."

Was it a dream? Had I started hearing strange voices? Certainly not! *We hadn't told anyone we needed more money for our travel. This has got to be God,* I pondered, as a myriad of questions swirled in my mind. Amid the swirls, however, were ripples of gratitude and praise to an omnipotent God. The week-long silence had been broken. The Lord had released one more piece of the puzzle. The remaining pieces were still whirling somewhere out there in space. We received just one piece at a time. The piece that said "destination" was yet to be discovered.

The day came and the money was released. Don held the unopened envelope in his hand and expressed pure gratitude to God for His gracious provision. He opened the envelope—cautiously, and was amazed at another mysterious, yet sweet surprise. Enclosed was a check of one thousand dollars, plus two fifty-dollar bills: total—one thousand one hundred dollars! *But why did it seem so specific—two fifty-dollar bills?* We'd been given another piece of our mysterious puzzle. The remaining pieces the Lord would reveal to us days to come. We sensed that something wonderful was about to happen.

4.

The Invisible GPS

"Whether you turn to the right or to the left, your ears will hear a voice behind you, saying, 'This is the way; walk in it'" (Isaiah 30:21, NIV).

"Don't be afraid to trust God; He will always be with you."
–Timothy Robinson

Mid-Atlantic Or Midwest?

Don's Dilemma

Recognizing and believing in the journey that God was calling us to take, Don resigned his job without knowing how or when he would pick up another one. We knew this was the right thing to do, as we had seen all God's revelations and miraculous interventions from the onset. We felt His peace. With all indications, it'd seemed that the Lord was leading us to Michigan. We had been told that Michigan would be a great place to raise young children. But with its economic downturns, Don's chances of getting a job there that would pay him enough to take care of his family were very slim. In fact, Michigan had one of the highest rates of unemployment in the United States. There were times when we argued with the Lord about that. It was difficult to understand why the Lord would choose a seemingly barren land as His first fruit to offer us.

During one of our questionings, we decided to peruse one of our religious organization's websites where education jobs would normally be posted. We found a job! A perfect fit for Don. This job was located in Maryland in one of our church schools. Since Don had talked with representatives in the Department of Pastoral Ministry at Michigan Conference about the possibility of obtaining a job and had gotten no encouraging word, we thought this new discovery had got to be the one. We looked at the qualifications and requirements and all spoke directly to Don's training and experience. Perfect! "Maybe the Lord meant Mid-Atlantic and not Midwest. At least they both begin with an M," we bantered.

Don spent hours—until midnight—answering all the essay questions, updating his resume, and writing personal statements that were required to complete the application process. Although we were still in the process of packing and tying up loose ends, we thought this was the job that would be worth the sacrifice of a couple hours. By midnight the application was off to its destination, and we hoped to hear good news.

The next morning, at approximately nine fifteen, Don had a message on his cell phone waiting for him! It was from the academy. We were very thrilled that everything was finally coming together and that we wouldn't have to eke out a living if we went to Maryland. Don returned the call promptly while I kept on packing and detaining the kids in the downstairs area to avoid feeding noise into their dad's telephone conversation. Don spoke with the administrative assistant who was quite jovial and understanding. A telephone interview was scheduled for Don to "meet" with the principal at approximately one o' clock in the afternoon on that day.

Don got dressed (in office clothes). He checked his phone to ensure it was working well, and then chose a quiet spot in our upstairs bedroom as his make-shift office. The kids and I prepared lunch and checked on Don periodically as he waited nervously for the call. But the unthinkable happened! He waited ... and waited ... and waited. One o'clock, two o'clock ... the call never came. *Very odd*, I thought. Don contacted the principal's office and was told that the principal had been very busy, but that they could have the interview later in the week—around Thursday.

In a few days we would set out on our journey not knowing whether it would be—Maryland or Michigan. We'd even applied to a graduate school in Michigan and felt certain that we would study for our doctorates ... but somehow the Lord had asked us to wait—the time had not been right. One thing we knew for sure: wherever the Lord led us would be just fine.

Husband. Kids. Luggage. All set! On the sunny afternoon of June 16, 2011, my family revved toward the resplendent glow of the western sun. Still embracing the possibility that the call for the interview would come in, we turned our eyes to what the Lord would reveal next.

Sunrise, Arizona

Driving over the hills of Arizona down to the flat lands of New Mexico aroused a feeling of relief and freedom. The mountainside, although somewhat scorched from the hot summer sun, swanked a hidden beauty that made itself visible to the appreciative eye. We made our first stop at Sunrise, Arizona. The Islas family welcomed us into their beautifully decorated home, where we would rest for the night. They took good care of us. Our hearts beat to the rhythm of gratitude for the kindness they'd shown.

Early the next morning, the warm tips of the sun's rays tapped me gently on my forehead as morning rolled up the covers of the night and tucked them away. I could smell the freshness of a brand new day, a new start. Time went by quickly as we shared light moments together with this wonderful family. Soon it was time to set out again on the next leg of our journey.

The small, navy-blue SUV had been parked by the curb, just outside the Islas' home. The truck seemed so ready as though it were calling us impatiently: "Come, let's get going." We took all our belongings we'd brought inside the home with us and placed then carefully in the very tightly packed U-Haul trailer. The clanking of the chain and the screaking of the trailer's door made everything sound so decisive—and it was!

The kids hopped into the crammed SUV excitedly, with no concern at all about space or clutter. They were ready! We buckled our children securely in their car seats. Then it was our turn to get comfortable in our own seats. Tucked under the front passenger seat were large paper and plastic bags stuffed with snacks, leaving just enough room to rest two adventurous feet. We settled in. Buckled up. And the engine roared. The Islas family stood in awe as they waved goodbye. We prayed, then drove off into the horizon. Homeless!

Where Is That Motel?

When we arrived at Flagstaff, Arizona, we went looking for a motel that Don had reserved. However, when we got there the strangest thing happened: We could not find the motel! Peering in the near distance, we could see a billboard with the motel's name written in bold letters.

"There it is.... I think I saw it just now," I said, feeling certain we had found the motel. But, we drove in front, behind and around the sign, and still could not locate the actual building. We laughed uncontrollably. Then it suddenly dawned on us: we did not ask the Lord where He wanted us to stay. In spite of all that God had revealed, we were still trying to work on our own agenda. It didn't work.

We gave up looking for the motel, as we believed the Lord was giving us a clear message in the "lost motel saga." A few minutes later, we spotted a fancy-looking motel that appeared a bit pricy. *Why would the Lord lead us to something we could barely afford?* I wondered. We felt a strong nudge. We stopped. Don opened the clean glass door and walked up to the desk. By now the kids had already fallen asleep, since we'd been traveling for more than three hours in the dark.

I peered curiously through the rolled up window of our SUV as Don approached my door. "Dear," he said, "they only have one room that someone has just cancelled while I was speaking with the receptionist—but it's a bit expensive. What do you think?"

We paused to pray, for we knew well that God's idea mattered most. "Let's take it." I said. We felt this was where the Lord wanted us to stay for the night for His reasons that He would later reveal. After this experience we chose not to reserve rooms, but to pray for the Lord to show us where He'd like us to sleep each night. And, miraculously, unseen hands guided us every night to the motel that had been hand-picked for my family.

Where Are Our Clothes?

The little people woke up when the cool Flagstaff wind caressed their tiny faces. They seemed tired, and we were, too. We placed one weary leg in front of the other, up the winding staircase to the last room our Guide had reserved. I slid the key with weary fingers into the door while holding my sleeping two-year-old daughter on my left arm. After we got the children settled in for the night, we rummaged through our "hand luggage" for clothes we'd wear the next day. "What happened to all our clothes we packed for the journey?" Don and I asked almost simultaneously.

"Ugh, what are we going to do?" I muttered. We reluctantly accepted the reality of wearing the same outer clothing for the next six days! Thank God underwear was available, since we had packed small pieces of clothing in various bags and suitcases. Our casual-wears were in another small suitcase that had been tucked all the way to the back of the trailer mistakenly—and impossible to retrieve. The kids were fortunate. They had enough clothes for the rest of the journey.

This experience had taught us a very vital lesson: We did not (and do not) need a closet full of clothes to be happy. Life can be beautiful with just enough. Less is more. We did not have access to all our clothes, but what was most important was that we were together as a family—a happy family. Scripture encourages that we should "not worry about tomorrow, for tomorrow will worry about itself. Each day has enough trouble of its own" (Matthew 6:34). Don and I could have been sour for the entire trip, but our desire for the mundane was overshadowed by the sacredness of our divine mission. We chose joy.

The Elusive Gas Station, Amarillo, Texas

The orange, yellow and pink sky faded into a dark shade of grey. We knew that another day had come to an end, and so was our energy. It was time to rest. "Lord, please show us where you'd like us to sleep tonight," we prayed. A quick glance at the gas gage alerted us that the van too was low on energy. It needed gas.

"Should we search for a motel first or go straight to the gas station and fill the tank?" Don and I negotiated. We prayed the Lord would tell us what to do as He'd always done. We wanted a very affordable motel, and the prices that we'd seen so far were a bit expensive.

Go to the gas station first, the now familiar voice said. So we headed in the direction of a sign in the distance marked—gas station.

We drove around, but just couldn't seem to find the gas station—even though the sign had seemed within eye shot. Sounds familiar? This was an experience we'd had before. God tended to hide one thing that seemed so obvious in order to reveal another. Eventually, we found ourselves in the opposite direction of the gas station. "How could this be?" we marveled. Surveying the area, we noticed that a grassy island separated the streets, which made it impossible for motorists to make U-turns. There were no shortcuts. However, this apparent lostness helped us make an incredible discovery.

Right there, exactly across from where we stopped, stood a beautifully erected building—a motel! We'd literally been led to the motel that the Lord had chosen for us that evening by obeying the voice that instructed us to go to the gas station first! You see, if we had found the gas station, most certainly we would have missed seeing this motel. Isn't God amazing? We laughed with hearts filled with wonderment and gratitude. That motel had been the cheapest and cleanest we'd seen on our whole trip. With such an affordable price, however, Don and I couldn't help but wonder if there'd been bed bugs waiting to hitch a free ride. But why this thought when God Himself had made His pick? We quickly redirected our thoughts and asked God to fulfill whatever His divine purpose was in that motel.

"Here you go, Sir," the receptionist said with a smile as he handed the key to Don. We headed to the room.

"The room is beautiful!" the kids remarked.

Everything was spic-and-span, quite efficient ... and no bed bugs—at least we didn't see any.

After we settled in our room, we all hopped into the car and headed to the gas station that, this time around, was easy to find. We'd even found a large supermarket a few blocks away—our evening meal had been taken care of as well.

You see, when we pray, we should be careful to keep in mind that our prayers may not get answered in the exact way we anticipated. The Lord may take us on detours, which ultimately will bring us back to the center of His will to grant us our hearts' deepest desires. He will give you what you need ... and then some.

5.

Protection And Confirmation

"... He will command his angels concerning you to guard you in all your ways" (Psalm 91:11, NIV).

"Fix your eyes on the chasm of difficulties and you may feel like you are falling in. Set your gaze on the view of hope and the journey will seem less daunting and more captivating." – *Dionne Robinson*

Confirmed! Tulsa, Oklahoma

It had been only weeks that several powerful tornadoes barreled through the flat terrains of Tulsa, Oklahoma. Inevitably, we would have to drive through this city, hoping we wouldn't be carried away by an unforeseen twister. Looking over the wide expanse of farm lands that connected with the horizon beyond, the kids and I admired the rich, green grass that created a gorgeous carpet strewed across the meadow. Tiny spring flowers added a magnificent, colorful design.

We drove through Oklahoma City en route to Tulsa. Everywhere seemed strangely calm, no visible signs of destruction. But something was in the air. Within every mile or so, there was a big, black electronic billboard flashing warnings of a looming thunderstorm—a severe one. *Please keep us safe, Lord,* I prayed silently. We breathed a sigh of relief when we found a motel, a cozy one, on the country side.

The kids had been excited to see all the new fixtures that'd been recently installed in the motel room: new bathroom, sink, carpet—everything. They jumped from bed to bed like they would a trampoline. Then, moments later there was a clap of thunder, a swift flash of lighting zipped across the sky. Down came the rain as though it were thrown from a gigantic pitcher, accompanied by strong gusts of wind. The thunderstorm had begun.

"Are we going to have a tornado, Mommy?" Timmy asked curiously.

I must confess that there had been a knot in my stomach. I'd been a bit nervous since there wasn't a basement that we could dive into in the event of a tornado. It's no joke being stranded in Tornado Alley. I swallowed hard and organized my thoughts.

"No, Son. I don't think so," I responded, sporting a look of bravado, "we'll be all right."

Not wanting to miss a single report, Don turned on the television. All four of us kept glued to the weather channel for up-to-date forecasts. My eyes drooped. But I just couldn't bring myself to falling asleep—not yet. "Father, please watch over us and keep us safe," I whispered. Before completing my sentence, the meteorologist said something, something rather interesting that caught our attention.

Quite mysteriously, the meteorologist pointed a bony finger directly at us, and said, "And Oklahoma, you will be all right, especially *you*, in Tulsa." Was he giving us a message of comfort from God? We didn't know. But one thing we knew for sure was that, this message brought peace, full serenity of the soul. Right then, we switched off the television. We felt safe. God had brought us comfort. The one question that kept on coming back had nothing to do with tornadoes, but everything to do with the destination the Lord had in mind for us.

Early the next morning, we woke up from a sweet sleep. The sun had woken up too and had started extending its long rays, as if to embrace the earth. It had been a perfect day to fall on our knees before our God Who had kept us safe.

"Father, here we are in Oklahoma, trusting your divine leadership. We know you are with us ... but we don't know where you would like us to go. Where do you want us to go from here? Please make it clear. Should we go to Maryland to seek out the job since they'd wanted to interview Don, or should we continue the journey to Michigan? Direct us," I petitioned.

Moments after praying, Don, the kids and I got off our knees. Don felt impressed to fetch his cell phone. He turned it on. There was a message awaiting him. "Who could this be?" Don wondered out loud. The kids and I sat up in eager anticipation to hear from the one who'd been appointed to give us a message, a clue to finding the next puzzling piece of the puzzle. "Hi Don," a crisp, clear voice said, "could you bring an avocado mascara for me when you are coming to Berrien Springs?" Now, Berrien Springs is in Michigan and not Maryland.

"Avocado mascara? Berrien Springs?" Don and I repeated simultaneously. That's kind of odd that a girl would ask a boy to get that kind of stuff. It was the voice of our dear friend, Gina, who had worked temporarily at the Mission School, where Don had taught for six years. Then, another piece of information we later received also solidified—even more fully in our hearts—where God was taking us. Unbeknown to us, Gina had also lived in Tulsa, Oklahoma, the very city we'd received confirmation for our destination! Don and I looked at each other. We smiled—this time with a deeper sense of purpose. We knew the answer had finally come in a very unusual, but God-directed manner.

"Let's get ready," Don said, "we are going to Michigan!" But why the deafening silence from Maryland? We had been looking forward to going to Maryland much more than we'd anticipated going to Michigan. You see, Michigan to us had seemed more like an unfruitful land, not the Promised Land. There were no jobs awaiting us there, not even an interview. Yet that was the place God chose for my family. An unsolved mystery it was, until it all came together.

Dear friend, when you pray, keep your eyes and ears open for God's *unusual* responses. Are you on an unconventional journey with God? Well, you might be the one "chosen to explain to everyone this mysterious plan that God, the Creator of all things, had kept secret from the beginning" (Ephesians 3:9).

The Receptionist: Collinsville, Illinois

Driving away from a sea of traffic we edged toward the horizon, one that a few months ago had seemed unattainable was now within our grasps. God had made the seemingly impossible, possible. My family felt gratefully overwhelmed with God's presence and promise. One final layover ... and then we'd head toward the Promised Land, a place the kids and I'd never seen. *It's a great place to raise young children,* our friends voices echoed in my mind. *It's the fruit basket of America.* Riding on these recommendations, I felt no concern or fear for what lay ahead.

Our next stop: Collinsville, Illinois. We felt God had not arranged a stopover in Missouri for reasons He would reveal at the appropriate time. As soon as we arrived in Collinsville, we knew it was the city for a stopover. God would confirm this even more as we approached the motel. The first appointed angel was one of the motel's receptionists named Pam—a very thoughtful woman, medium build, with long, honey-blond hair. My husband went into the motel first while the children and

I waited in the van. Upon his return, Don announced: "Our room will be on the third floor." Somehow I was hoping for a room on the first floor since we had two young children. I accepted and placed my concerns in God's hands. But, interestingly, as the children and I walked toward the motel, I noticed that Pam, the receptionist, was standing by the window with a glow on her face, gazing at us. As soon as Don opened the door, Pam said, "I am going to rebook you for a room on the first floor, instead of the third floor. The room has just been cleaned and the floor is still a bit wet." We expressed our gratitude, for we knew it came from the Father's hand. One thing we'd learned throughout the journey was to accept and embrace change—even last minute ones. Why? We knew God had our back.

Pam showed us to our room (a large suite one would expect to see in a five-star hotel). I could scarcely believe I was in a motel. She spread blankets over the damp floor and made sure we were comfortable before returning to her desk. It was as though she were appointed to be extra caring and kind to us.

During our conversation we mentioned that we were relocating to Michigan from California. Pam found this information mind-boggling. She couldn't understand why anyone would leave California with all the glitter and glamor (a place she dreamed of visiting) to go to the woods of Michigan. Her concerns gave us a window of opportunity to do something special. We shared our faith and a few testimonies of what God had been doing for our family. From the look on Pam's face, I believe something miraculous had started to take root in her heart. She wished us God's blessing.

The next morning we woke up feeling refreshed. We gathered our belongings ... and waved goodbye while our car disappeared behind small, slender maple trees. Feelings mounted as we departed the motel's parking lot in Collinsville. This would have been the last, the very last stopover before entering the Land of Promise. We drove five or six hours, with a few pit stops. In the sky, huge clouds gathered as the sun dipped behind the Midwestern horizon. The lush, green trees that lined both sides of the busy street swayed gently in the wind, as if to say, *Welcome home.* The Promised Land—at last! The end of a seven-day journey. New hopes. New realities. New people. New divine appointments.

The Promised Land

By now the sun had already draped its curtains over the small Michigan town. Outside was pitch black, too dark to see much of anything. Only nocturnal fireflies blinking among clusters of trees like Christmas lights strewn in a dark room. As we emerged from the duskiness, glares of florescent lights hit our eyes. The dim lights casted shadows over well-manicured lawns on the beautiful campus of Andrews University. We desired to drive around the gorgeous compound, but we needed rest. It was time to retire from our very long journey.

Amazingly, the kids were still awake, for, they too, had been eager to see the Promised Land. We found a modest motel suitable for the night. Never before had we slept like we did that night, leaning on the big shoulders of a trust-worthy God. As we slumbered, God spoke in a peculiar way. I had a dream—a vision it would be. Something made this dream stand out. Interestingly, the story occurred within the context of the brand-new city we'd just settled in. Usually, the setting of my dreams would be centered on my childhood community or some other very familiar location. It would normally take months for a new location to show up in my dreams. But this time (for the first time), it was different. I had a dream that was more than a dream.

The setting? Andrews University cafeteria—a place I'd never even visited before. Yet, in my dream, I saw myself dining in the university's cafeteria. Sitting at one of the tables was a student who appeared somewhat distraught. I walked up to her and placed my arm around her shoulder. "What's wrong?" I asked. The young woman spoke between tears while she poured out her heart to me. With my arm still resting on her shoulder, I spoke words of comfort to her.

The powerful impact of this dream lingered in my heart ... for a very long time, and I knew it was a direct message from the Lord. I could hardly wait to share with Don what had transpired that night. Throughout the entire trip, we petitioned for one important revelation: the ministry God would hand-pick for us. The answer came—not at the other six motels we did our layovers, but at the seventh motel, our final destination, the very first night on its soil.

"Hon, I know what the Lord wants me to do," I shared with my dear husband.

"Hmm, what did your Father reveal to you?" Don asked with interest.

"He wants me to be involved in the ministry of comfort," I said as I chomped on a piece of vegetable pizza.

There was no doubt in my mind that this was the path God had laid out for me. It was clear. You see, Don and I had dedicated our talents—from as early as our brains would allow us to recall. We performed in religious services, accepting every office we'd been nominated to fill: elder, superintendent, teacher, secretary, family life director—you name it, and we'd say, *We've done that.* But on this new journey, I'd been personally impressed to steer clear of that path ... and be more intimately involved in personal ministries—reaching people where they are.

Since that dream, there hadn't been a day that the Lord had not brought someone along my way: someone to encourage, someone to comfort. He'd also anointed me to write, a major pipeline to pour words of comfort into open hearts. This revelation had only been the tip of the iceberg, however. What we discovered next would absolutely blow our minds and break the journey's puzzle into pieces, then swirl the fragments around like leaves caught in a whirlwind, pulling each section back together to spell not just faith, but gratitude.

For the next two days, we were led to the Andrews campus to stay two nights in the dormitory. I even ate at the cafeteria to familiarize myself with the place God had used to form an important context for my ministry. It felt holy. Later in the day we roamed the campus, taking pictures of every pretty thing we laid our eyes on. The landscape? Breath-taking. We really felt like we had made it to the city God had chosen.

At the dorm—after a long day—Don, being very adept at math, started calculating the cost of the whole trip. Our discovery made us want to scream real loud, but we couldn't, since we were afraid that the dorm officials would run to our rescue to save us from—well, ourselves. In an earlier chapter in this book, I'd mentioned that God had provided miraculously a one-thousand-dollar check and two fifty-dollar bills. He'd also given us an additional fifty-dollar bill through a kind colleague. These fifty-dollar bills, along with the one-thousand-dollar check had appeared to have a mystery surrounding them, so we kept track of our spending, keeping all receipts. We had wondered often: *Why so specific, why three fifty-dollar bills*? but left an open end for the Lord to reveal the answer in His time.

Well, do you want to know the amazing truth? The last three fifty-dollar bills were to cover the costs for the last three nights we would spend at the dorm at Andrews University. All in all, the one-thousand-dollar check and three fifty-dollar bills given to us specifically for the journey had turned out to be the exact amount of money needed to cover the entire trip from California! Although others had given us monetary gifts, it was clear that the three fifty-dollar bills and the one-thousand-dollar check were for the Lord's journey. We had used the money just as we'd been instructed by its donors—a gift to be used for the journey.

Now, it was all clear. God had directed us to a no-motel stay in Missouri. Had we not obeyed and stopped in Missouri, the money would not have been sufficient to cover our trip as was divinely designed. We'd stopped in all the states we'd driven through, but when we got to Missouri, the Lord said, *Keep going*. And, if we'd found the "lost motel" in Flagstaff, Arizona, and had not stayed at the pricy one we'd been led to, the total would not have been accurate. Oh, what a mighty God!

Beyond the shadow of a doubt, we knew God was with us, and still is. Whenever our kids speak, they also do with this knowledge and acknowledge God for His great provisions. Our hearts swelled with joyful elation at the supernatural interventions and provisions of a gracious God! Is there anything too hard for God! Most certainly not!

6.

Dirty Deliverance

(Three Months Later)

"He grants the desires of those who fear Him; He hears their cries for help and rescues them" (Psalm 145:19, NLT).

"No matter how big you think your problem is, it is still no match to the size of your God. He will do what He says He will do."
– *Dionne Robinson*

Saved By the Sewer

Seven days of travel across country had left us exhausted. We were ready for our own home, our very own beds. We hoped to find a nice, spacious apartment. Instead, we got something we never dreamed of: a very small basement apartment. *This has got to be a joke*, I thought. We believed God had reserved a big, beautiful, fully-furnished apartment for us, since He had instructed us to leave all our furniture behind. As a family we had never lived in a small space like this one, let alone a basement. With shoulders drooped, we took it anyway, trusting God's leading as we knew He hadn't abandoned us.

We moved in—with no furniture. The first few days we spread blankets on the king-size floor bed. I cried. But I never lost hope in the One Who had been faithful. By the end of the first week, it really started to feel like home. "Not bad after all," I'd sometime banter. Then, we got an upgrade—a big sofa bed! During the day it served as a chair and table; at night, a bed. Throughout this bumpy experience, we felt our Father's shoulders rubbing against our heads, while He took us through the test.

I looked at my children as they giggled delightfully in a corner in the tiny apartment, and thought, *You are worth every bit of this sacrifice.* The King of kings did this for us, His children. He left His comfortable heavenly abode, journeyed to an uncomfortable world that rejected Him ... lived uncomfortably, just to introduce us to a better life. Thank you, Jesus! Are we better than the King of the Universe? Of course not. Make no mistake, though, this was, by no means, a walk in the park. But trusting God's leading, staying focused, and not worrying about impressing anyone gave us inner strength and courage to stay on our journey with our Guide.

As the days went by and we started to explore, we got the opportunity to meet our neighbors who had been very warm and welcoming. This day-to-day greeting, however, would lead us to a wonderful discovery. The Morrises were our compatriots. (This was exciting for us as our children had never had the opportunity to live among their parents' countrymen). The Morrises also had a vegetable garden with indigenous foods we'd long desired. We'd always wanted to introduce these foods to our children. Amazingly, this too, the Lord had taken into consideration. Our small apartment had become a launching pad that catapulted us into a community of caring compatriots. Deep down, however, we knew that it wouldn't be long before we'd have to say goodbye to these wonderful people—as neighbors. Our daughter had started having serious allergic reactions in the small basement apartment, and we knew we had to leave—fast!

Our mountain-top experience would quickly zip-line into a valley encounter. Disappointment settled like a fog over our apartment. Depression, too, was moving in. We'd anticipated getting a bigger and more beautiful home. But the Lord did the reverse. He gave us something that in the flesh we would not have chosen—only through His Spirit. We knew also that we had to stay in this apartment, since it was not at all feasible to pick up something more sophisticated until our stringent budget had more room for flexibility.

Soon Don would get a job, one that the Lord Himself had miraculously chosen for him exactly two months after our arrival. There was a ray of hope. Finding a bigger apartment quickly became a new topic of interest. Would we be able to move? With one salary that had been slashed in half ... and no longer reflected the California salary scale, things had become tight. In spite of this slight inconvenience, however, we agreed not to second-guess what God had been doing. He had revealed enough to us to strengthen our faith. So why doubt Him now?

The story of the Children of Israel crossing the Red Sea—a miraculous manifestation of God's power—and how they doubted God shortly thereafter stood at the forefront of my mind. *I cannot doubt my God,* I assured my faith, *He has been too good to us and had proven Himself faithful.* But each time my little girl had an allergy attack of any kind, I'd worry.

In fact, Arielle's allergies had gotten even worse, and we were still unable to locate an apartment right away, one that was beautiful enough and fit within our budget. We prayed. We waited for an answer. We prayed. We waited. We felt stuck between a rock and a hard place and wondered when our Rock (Jesus) would come through for us. Amidst the anxiety and frustration, we knew that our deliverance would come—at the right time, but when? Something strange was in the air, and it made me nervous.

The Fateful Friday

On one fateful evening, the proverbial straw broke the camel's back! Don had already left for work. I was busy at home with my usual before-sun-down routines. Suddenly, I noticed something different about my little girl. She'd started to regurgitate. She appeared lethargic, falling asleep often. Things had taken a down turn. That was it! "Lord, we need out now," I exclaimed with a sense of helplessness. How much more could we endure, especially now that our kids' well-being was at stake? *Sickness had never been an issue for our children, so why now,* I wondered. What's more, Don had started his new job just a little over one month and health insurance hadn't yet kicked in. Taking a break from my self-pity party, I got an idea—a bright one that quickly faded.

I felt inspired to take the kids outside. I did. Right away our little girl got well—but not for long. As soon as we got back inside, everything started where they'd left off. From this unpleasant situation, the children would poke fun, saying: "We go outside—yay! Feel better! We come back inside—aah, sick!" The kids knew how to turn the most challenging situation into a subject of play and humor. They'd been built for the mission.

While we continued to pray for deliverance from our plight, the answer came in a totally unexpected manner. Don had left for work that Friday morning, as usual, with plans to stop at the grocery store to pick up ingredients for the family's weekly special (sweet potato pudding) on his way home. "Dear, could you pick up a plunger at the store?" I asked, "our toilet is clogged and I'm afraid it might overflow onto the floor."

Little did we realize that this very unpleasant circumstance would be the beginning of the deliverance we so desperately needed. Not long after the first call for the plunger, a second call went out—this time with more urgency.

"Dear, could you come home right away? Smelly sewage water is all over the floor ... in the closet, everywhere!" Don hurried home, wanting to make sure his family was okay. The grime moved slowly—with a peculiar effect over the floor. The sun crept behind the horizon. We desired the sweet Sabbath rest we'd hoped for all week! Now the decision was obvious: we had to make a quick exit. But where would we go?

Helping Hands

We summoned the Morrises, who were just a block away. They lovingly came to our rescue, helping us secure our belongings and moving anything that was at risk of being contaminated by the grimy water to their house. We stowed the rest of our possessions at a safe spot (on the stairs that led outside the walk-out basement apartment), where we would return to retrieve them on Sunday. We spent the next two nights at our neighbors' until we received further instructions from our Master Guide.

Amidst the stench and frustration, there was a sweet sense of God's presence. We knew that He had answered our prayers—in an unusual way. Not only did we move out of the apartment, our landlord had also refunded our security deposit, paving the way for another miracle several months later.

7.

Appointed Angels

"For God is not unjust. He will not forget how hard you have worked for Him and how you have shown your love to Him by caring for other believers, as you still do" (Hebrews 6:10, NLT).

"Give praises to God because He is great and wonderful."
– *Timothy Robinson*

The Gracious Heart of a Town Mother

After the dirty deliverance from our basement apartment, my body was still in shock. But there was no time to throw a pity party. We needed an apartment—fast! We checked everywhere possible, where apartment ads could be found, but still nothing of interest. We had just two days to find an apartment—and day one had already passed. *Where would the Lord lead us next?* Since we were relatively new to the area, there had been a feeling of lostness. There hadn't been enough time to feel truly settled. And with two preschoolers, moving had never been easy—for us, that is. Amazingly, our three-year-old daughter and our five-year-old son seemed perpetually excited, their inner peace undisturbed. Every situation had been an adventure for them. They'd gladly go wherever the Lord led their parents. "God will provide," we'd assure them, and they believed with all their tiny hearts.

As the Saturday evening sun disappeared sluggishly behind thick, grey clouds, so was our attempt to find an apartment. Finding suitable housing on this side of town had always been a challenge. Nevertheless, we resolved to keep hope and faith alive. God had started us on a new phase in our faith-walk, something for which I'd not been prepared—something I did not anticipate.

We'd received a few offers from members of our church who had short-term rentals, but these wouldn't be available right away. Then, I got a strong impression from the Lord to speak with Audrey Payne, a wonderful lady Don and I had met earlier. I picked up the telephone.

"Audrey, do you know of anyone who might have an apartment that is move-in ready?" I enquired.

"... I think I know someone I could ask," Audrey responded

Moments later Audrey telephoned me back with good news! She'd found someone—Novlin Coleman, who'd turned out to be a friend of a long-time friend we had in California. Weeks later, I also discovered that this dear lady knew two of my favorite professors: Dr. Hyacinth Rose and Mr. Ralston Rose.

I felt very hopeful. What's more, Novlin had been a business woman, the owner of good-looking apartments. During this predicament, however, none of her apartments was available. Graciously, Novlin made an offer, one that would involuntarily resurrect memories that had long been buried. *Why was God bringing me back to this juncture?* I pondered. Knots squeezed tighter in the pit of my stomach when the answer did not come.

"She's like a town mother," one neighbor remarked.

"She's as sweet as honey," another person affirmed. But how could I accept her loving offer to stay in her home until we found an apartment?

"This journey is getting a bit odd," Don and I would say. For the kids, they had been bubbling with enthusiasm. It would have been another motel stop—in their world.

How Will I Do This, Lord?

After wrestling with the Lord, we accepted to do what He had ordained as part of His plan. This was clearly God's way and not ours. Some friends from our church, Brian and Larry, came by early that Sunday morning and helped us move our belongings to the Coleman's residence. It had been a wet, windy and chilly morning, and my eyes and heart weren't much different. *How on earth am I going to do this, Lord?* I kept on asking. By now the rain from the outside seemed to have suddenly started falling from my eyes. I wept—bitterly, as though something or someone special had been ripped away from me. I felt helpless. I sat glued to my seat in the car, refusing to go.

Sensing my struggle, the gracious town mother approached the passenger side of the car where I'd been throwing a huge pity party. As Novlin spoke words of comfort to me, I could feel her love, her caring heart, her authenticity. Her smile drove the rain clouds away and suddenly something mysterious happened in my heart. Then, a voice inside me said, "You must go. Let go of your past hurts and trust Me."

"How am I going to do this, Lord? I didn't come to the Promised Land for this," I protested. I pictured myself as a goat that the Lord was trying to coax, pull, coax and pull. But I knew my Father too well. I had to obey. My son, Timothy, patted me gently on my back, and said, "It's going to be all right, Mommy. See, Mommy, Arielle and I are happy. We like it." What great encouragement that was to my heart.

For a brief moment I was transported back to my teenager years, where I'd been emotionally abused while living with extended family, and I'd vowed never to set foot in another person's house, other than my own.

As Brian and Larry pulled our last suitcases into the well-kept house, the scratching sound of the wheels jolted me back to my present reality. *This is it*, I thought, *It'll be interesting to see God's reason behind this.*

Larry, a friend from our church, who had been kind to help us move, remarked, "This woman is as sweet as honey. I think you will be all right."

And Larry was right. This wonderful woman, Novlin Coleman, along with her husband, Roy, welcomed us joyfully. Later we would make an interesting discovery.

Novlin shared that she'd been praying to have children around her. She had a special love for children, a love I admired. After her own children had grown and taken on adult responsibilities, footprints of emptiness had marked her hallways; no more patter of tiny feet– until my kids arrived!

Our kids loved Novlin dearly and she loved them, too. She'd become a loving aunt to them. Who knew that the Lord would've brought our family to this house as an answer to Novlin's prayer? She enjoyed having us around and the queasiness I'd had on the inside disappeared. Healing had started to take place. The shackles of the past fell with a clunk! This experience brought blessing that we'd never dreamed of.

The Green Drink!

After the first month in the Coleman's home, I observed Novlin's health-conscious approach to living. I loved it. However, I must confess that the first time she offered me a glass of *green drink* I could not allow myself to drink it, as I'd always thought that any drink that was green belonged to the goblins, not me. But my husband, Don, urged me to try it: "It's really delicious; take a sip."

The next morning I opened the fridge, and, behold, another green drink was sitting on the top shelf. It seemed like this drink knew my name. With all its mighty greenness it begged me to taste and see. I braced myself ... and ... took a big sip, preparing to sputter. But I didn't. Don was right! The smoothie was absolutely tasty!

Smoothies (and other natural foods) had been blended into my family's diet ... and we loved it! I'd even been impressed to follow in Novlin's footsteps in eating raw foods. The Lord had brought me to this home to bring healing to my own heart, to save my very life. And the blessing didn't stop there. It was at this home that I received a special revelation to write my first devotional book *Experiencing God in Everyday Ordinary Things: Big Lessons from Little People.* I am still amazed, still not able to explain how the aforementioned book could be written in just two months, while two energetic preschoolers climbed onto my chair and screamed in my ears. This was just another marvelous intervention of a mighty God.

The Lord had brought us to the Coleman's to experience the powerful involvement of the Holy Spirit in inexplicable ways. We spent three months there—three marvelous months!

Hello, Downstairs!

It felt right. It had been almost three months at the Coleman's, and we sensed God had accomplished His plan. Initially, we thought the house-to-house pilgrimage that we'd been prodded into was for us to be a blessing to the household. But one day God gave us a glimpse of His divine plan—it was for us, not for them! This revelation became more powerful after we moved to our next location—our third home within six months!

As is customary, every time we moved to a new home, we'd ask the Lord to reveal to us His divine purpose for bringing us to that particular place. We'd come to accept that God wasn't leading us on our own terms, but on His. This felt somewhat uncomfortable since, as a family, we liked to feel settled and have everything well organized in our own home. This time, however, the Lord had decided to do it His way.

We'd learned about an apartment approximately five miles out of town. Dr. Tom Wilson, who had also been a member of our church, contacted us to let us know that he had a downstairs apartment available. At the time when the offer was made, we felt the time wasn't right for the transition. We waited until we got the green light from our Master Guide. When He did, we knew the time was perfect. I picked up the phone and dialed the number I had secured.

"Come on over and take a look at the apartment and see if you like it," Tom said politely. That same day we headed out, using the directions we'd received over the phone. We had a little run around, but eventually, we found it—an eye-catching house. On the outside, we liked the landscape—just gorgeous! On the inside, we fell in love with its interior design that revealed character and charm.

"What do you think?" Tom asked.

"Suits us well," we responded.

The children, too, were delighted. There was one concern, however. There was a pond in the backyard. *"What if the kids wandered to the pond and—?"* my thoughts were interjected with an invitation to see the upstairs, where Tom's beautiful wife, Marlene, was waiting with a twinkle in her eye. Funny enough, she continued the conversation as though she had gotten a peak into my mind. She told us about the pond and how concerned one mother who had lived in a nearby cottage on the property was, how the mother would panic whenever she lost sight of her kids. Fortunately, nothing unfavorable happened. The dark-green water, partly sheeted with green pond weeds looked somewhat intimidating. For us, we'd been lucky to be there at the start of winter, which meant the pond would be frozen for months. Although it was a short-term arrangement, it felt great. And, we took comfort in knowing that the safest place to be was in the will of God.

In a matter of days the Wilsons would leave for their vacation in California—the place from which we'd relocated. What's more, they trusted us to stay at their home—such gesture is called divine favor. In their absence, we made sure everything was well taken care of and looked forward to seeing them again in three weeks. Their arrival marked a new phase of our journey.

"Hello, downstairs," a deep voice called from upstairs.

"Hello, upstairs," Don greeted.

Every day, for the two months we'd been there, our kind neighbor would check on us as he would his own children. Our kids took to Tom quickly ... and before long, they were playing chase. What fun times they would have together.

The Walk on the Trail

One day, in the dead of winter, the temperatures mysteriously climbed up to the fifties. In Michigan, this means a hot day, unlike us in Southern California who'd be sporting turtle-neck sweaters and scarves in such temperatures. It didn't take us long to learn to go light when it hit the fifties—even if we had to grit our teeth a bit. This day was simply gorgeous, which would make enjoying the outdoors a worthy venture.

"Let's take the kids for a walk," Tom suggested.

"Sounds like a plan," I agreed.

Not hesitating, the kids and I hopped into Tom's big, brown truck and drove across the street, where tall trees enclosed an enchanting hiking trail. Snow hugged the root of the trees, extending its white powdery substance across the narrow path. With each step the sharp, crunchy sound of ice gave us a chilly reminder that winter was not about to bid us farewell—at least, not yet. We walked and talked. Cleverly, Tom told us the names of strange-looking plants, and, at times, asked us to guess the names of interesting hoof prints. Lost on the trail of pleasantries, time went by faster than we could keep track. Soon it was time to return home. The kids could not wait to tell tales of their walk on the trail to their dad.

After the hike on that cool winter day, something amazing happened inside of me.

A Father's Heart

"I think I've found a father," I shared with Don. Footprints of joy had been imprinted all over my face. As a young child (about six years old) I'd lost my daddy, so I never knew what it was really like to have an earthly dad. (My heavenly Father is the only Father I ever knew.) My pop had passed away from chronic asthma. A hellish suffering I had witnessed at a young age. I couldn't stand hearing the cries of my father. I felt helpless. He suffered so much. I can remember hearing him pray out loud for the Lord to let him die, especially when it became too difficult for him to breathe, and the nebulizer ceased to be effective. Then one day, the unthinkable happened? My dear father died—right beside me, while I slept in my parents' bed. That picture of my father is still fresh in my memory to this day.

I'd often wished I had a father with whom I could share my hopes and fears—someone who'd be strong enough to listen and understand where it hurts most. The absence of my father had made me feel vulnerable, not having someone to stand in my defense. But this time around, I saw a father in this man whom I'd just met. What's more, we shared the same last name. After sharing these thoughts with Don, I cautioned: "Please don't tell Tom; I'll just enjoy his fatherly heart remotely."

Every day for almost three months, Tom would go an extra mile to show how much he cared. One afternoon he did something I did not anticipate.

He came by the apartment (downstairs), and said, "I'm on my way outside. Do you have any trash you'd like me to take out?"

I'd always known Tom was a good man, but this kind gesture had made him a greater man. I saw Jesus in him. He was totally big on the inside!

The Frozen Pond

A few weeks earlier, the pond was dark and daunting. Now, it seemed inviting. I wanted to "walk on water." Sometimes, walking on water, however, could apply to a half-frozen pond—a risk no one wanted to take. One chilly morning, at approximately ten o' clock, I got another call from upstairs. It was the voice we'd always looked forward to hearing.

"Hello, downstairs! Would you like us to go sledding on the pond today?"

Like a real father, Tom, a retired surgeon, pulled a sled filled with three happy people around the pond that had been frozen hard. What a joy it was! I'd never had playful moments with a father—no, not ever in my life. I'd had mentors before, but this time was different.

Marlene, his dear wife, had also been a quiet source of strength. She'd often wonder how we were doing and if we had been feeling bored. She wanted us to be all right. One morning Marlene revealed her love in a special way. She prepared a delicious pancake batter with healthy fruit and nuts for us to give ourselves a breakfast treat. The timing could not have been more perfect. And when she chose a gift—whether a house-warming gift for me or birthday presents for the kids—she'd put considerable amount of thought into her selection. Our appreciation for this caring woman grew, making "parting a sweet kind of sorrow."

Leaving The Hill

The contract at the Wilson's residence had expired. It was time to say goodbye. As difficult as it was, we stayed brave, masking every hint of a tear. My heart broke a bit, as I felt the pain of parting. But, one thing I'd learned was that one should always stick to his or her word. We gave the Wilsons our word and two months it would be. We'd decided on two months since we had been looking into buying a house—a process that had mysteriously slipped into an "intertestamental period" (prophetic silence). But we knew better not to complain about the Lord's doing. He'd do it His way, in His time. We set out to our new home—our fourth!

Two months after settling into our new apartment, it dawned on me that something was missing. I'd missed hearing the familiar call "hello, downstairs." So I picked up the telephone and made a call to the Wilson's. Tom answered the phone. As if prophetic, during our conversation, Tom's words sounded God-directed. I'd never revealed to him my thoughts about desiring a father—not once. Yet, he spoke predictively.

As he shared fatherly words of wisdom, he interjected, "I am not afraid to call you my daughter.... You are a good person, and we also share the same last name. Feel free to talk with me anytime you need to."

How did he know what to say? Who put those words on His lips? The answer wasn't too obscure. Our heavenly Father has more than a thousand ways to grant His children their heart's desires. After all these years without an earthly father, the Lord knew now was the time—the stage where the loving, encouraging words of an earthly father would be appreciated. Why did God lead us to this beautiful home on the hill? What do you think?

8.

Hidden Treasures

(Testimonies of God's Miraculous Provisions)

"The LORD directs the steps of the godly. He delights in every detail of their lives" (Psalm 37:23, NLT).

"Many of life's most valuable treasures are often found in some of the most inauspicious places."
– *Don Robinson*

Bare Walls, Empty Spaces

It was approximately ten minutes past eight o'clock in the morning, Friday March 2. Don had just arrived home from work, exhausted. He had worked the night shift at the hospital (a simple arrangement that fit perfectly into the Master's plan). Being the terrific husband and loving father Don had always been, no sleep would be sweet until he found the right place for his family to live. Putting sleep aside—temporarily, Don drove into the parking lot of our soon-to-be apartment complex. The property manager was already there waiting for him.

Two months prior to this meeting, Don had walked through the very apartment we were about to lease. Little did he realize that when he was walking through this apartment that it would be the one he would someday call home. Responding to an ad at the Andrews University website, Don took interest in viewing the items advertised. During that brief encounter, the tenants gave Don a tour of the apartment—he walked through every room, not realizing that God was giving him a preview. The tenants left shortly thereafter, and the apartment became available.

"There hadn't been much interest ... until the week you telephoned me," the owner expressed.

Had God been preserving this apartment for us, I wondered. Despite the fact that other people had shown interest in the apartment, they'd never followed through. Our application was the first the landlord would receive. She assured us that as long as all background checks went well, the apartment would be ours. And it was definitely ours.

"Except for a few fixtures that need fixing, the apartment seems OK," Don reported. We had searched long and hard to find an apartment with similar amenities, but had been unsuccessful. We moved in.

But six months later, we would discover a creepy revelation. There had been creepy-crawlies living in the walls, as it was an older apartment that we'd rented. Moving to the country gave us not only the finest offerings of Mother Nature, but also the inevitable that country living offered: insects, rodents and arachnids. Was I prepared for this?

This encounter would gnaw at a memory that I'd packed away years ago. As a child growing up in the country—on a fifteen-acre property, punctuated with fruit trees of all varieties and origins—I'd encountered a similar outbreak. My modest childhood home—a home where my parents had raised their eight children, offered everything that accompanied country living. We didn't have plenty, but I would observe time and time again, my mom sharing from whatever little she had. We would polish the red wood floor until it glistened like a spotless mirror.

After my father lost his battle with chronic asthma, it became even tougher on my mother to provide for all of us. She'd told me how she would cut her own clothes to make dresses for us girls. She sacrificed everything to see us through the worse days. In spite of the struggles, older siblings and elders (and youth alike) of the small community would tell humorous stories in endless loops, which stirred thunderous belly laughs. People walked everywhere they went—sometimes more than six miles per day. I was not shielded from these daring treks, either. Getting to school on time was most daunting: There was only one bus, driven by a middle-aged man named Mr. P. Missing this bus meant that students had a slim chance to make it to school on time, if at all.

There were times when I would be running to catch the only bus, at five o' clock in the morning—alone, when I'd be ambushed by big dogs that would pounce out of nowhere and start chasing me. I'd run back to the direction that I had no intentions of retracing.

When the pursuit finally halted, I'd hear the only bus moaning as it climbed laboriously over the steep hill—without me. But one thing I knew, for sure, was that I was not going to retreat and go back home. I was determined to get to school, even if I had to ride with a total stranger. Giving up was not an option. I loved school. Even if it meant walking twelve miles, I'd be there. And that was the same determination my husband, Don, revealed as we later shared our stories.

Sometimes I'd wish I had company walking with me through the dark to help me get past the German Shepherds that roamed the winding roads in the wee hours of the morning. Even though we had nine dogs at home, still they were no match to these hounds. We had ordinary dogs, ones we'd sometimes call pencil tails.

There were also chickens running around freely in the yard, goats grazing on the jagged hill sides. Then, there were insects. All types of creepy-crawlies scuttling around like pets. Rats scampering on the roof, big lizards crawling intimidatingly on the walls. One could call it an "adventurous critter zoo." I was terrified of them. Relief came after I moved to the city to live with relatives. Soon I would forget all about my fear of rodents and creepy crawlies—until now. My nightmare had returned.

The rise of critters worsened in this apartment. Pest control came. They sprayed. They gelled. But nothing could stop the production of potentially destructive insects. Every time the pest exterminators came, we'd come down with allergic reactions to the chemicals used. It had seemed that we would probably die in the process while the critters lived on. We had only one remedy—moving. But we had six months left on the contract. Would we lose our deposit? Was there another apartment move-in ready before winter? We hoped to find a home more suitable for our family. Through this process, however, God did something amazing to my heart and brought me back to the day the apartment was secured.

I don't surprise myself often, but this time I sure did. How did this happen? Was I accepting an apartment I did not scrutinize thoroughly? Indeed, I was. (And I'm not crazy.) I would only see the apartment (for the first time) on the day we moved in. But I wasn't perturbed. The idea of *I'll have to see it first* had been diminished. Don would make the selection alone—with God. For this to have occurred, I knew God had truly done something marvelous in my heart. "How can I not trust the God Who had been leading my family miraculously, mysteriously, even," I affirmed. God had shown my family over and over again that He was capable of providing for our smallest and biggest needs. So, I trusted Him to select a place of residence for me.

Don signed the lease—to say the least. He picked up the keys for our new unfurnished home. But the big question was: how would we furnish it? All the previous apartments we'd lived at since relocating had been furnished—as we'd expected. In earlier chapters of this book, you'd probably recall how God had instructed us to leave all furniture ... and appliances behind in California. So when we arrived in Michigan, our interpretation was that God would *only* provide a place that had already been furnished. Were we in for a huge surprise! This apartment was empty! We had no furniture. But there was one thing we knew for sure: "Our God would meet all our needs according to His glorious riches in Christ Jesus" (Phil. 4:19).

Furniture ... And Then Some

When day dawned two days before we signed the lease for our new apartment, we had neither an apartment to move into nor furniture to fill the empty spaces. Despite the fact that God had proven Himself faithful, I'd started to feel overwhelmed. Doubt was creeping in. And I knew why: I wanted God to do it my way. I no longer wanted to depend on Him, for His method seemed too humbling for me—and I was mad. "God, I'm not too sure about this new way," I'd say, "is there another way?" Being the private, self-sufficient person I'd always been, I now felt vulnerable—an unwelcomed emotion.

But this would be only the beginning of the peeling process. Each day God would strip away, bit by bit—my pride, my independent streak. Half way through the process He would pause, then throw in a challenging test to see how well I'd been adjusting. It hurt badly. I'd scream, "Please, stop!" Kicking and screaming had only left me exhausted, too tired to resist. And as I drifted away into submission to the One Who knew me best and loved me most, something incredible began happening.

Through it all, Don kept a strong hold on faith and believed with all his heart that the Lord would provide in His unique way as He had before.

Then one day, approximately one week before we moved into our new, unfurnished apartment I got an e-mail from a dear lady named Kathie Lichtenwalter.

"I thought of you yesterday when I heard that DeEtta and John ... are moving to California. They have a lovely ... house on Long Lake Road [for sale]," Kathie wrote.

Don and I knew the Lord had steered us away from buying a house; nonetheless, I knew the Lord was up to something. So I asked Kathie if this family would be having a garage sale since they were relocating.

"I don't know," Kathie responded, "but here is their telephone number."

I dialed the number immediately. What I heard during this initial contact kept my mouth opened as though I'd suddenly lost the ability to keep it closed.

"Hello?" said a very pleasant voice.

"Um, (cleared my throat), Kathie mentioned to me that you'll be moving to California.... My family has just relocated from California," I added. "Do you think you'll be having a garage sale anytime soon?"

"... I would imagine that we'll be having a garage sale soon," DeEtta said, "is there something specific that you're looking for?"

But, what do I ask for when I need several pieces of furniture to furnish an empty apartment? I contemplated. "Well, um, I'm looking to furnish a new apartment my family will be moving into in the next few days."

"I think we have plenty of furniture you could use.... Feel free to come and take a look at them," DeEtta said most warmly. Did I just hear what I think I heard? Was God really doing this?

What a day! My heart cried tears of joy ... but lingering was a sense of embarrassment for doubting God's leading in my life. That beautiful evening we drove over—eagerly—to meet the family whom God had appointed.

When we arrived, the Chen family greeted us affably. This day felt like it was one the most important days in the history of my life. I knew I'd never be the same, for God was getting closer to the core of my heart, in His peeling process.

There was something special, something different about this beautiful family. Later Don and I would learn that the Chens too had been on an amazing journey with their God. They believed in the power of prayer, and they'd come to embrace unique divine encounters. No wonder God had hand-picked them to bless us—a lot! To confirm it all, God had one more step. Wanting to engrave His divine stamp, the Lord had impressed upon my heart to share the good news with Brian Manley—our head elder at the time, who had teamed up with Larry Woodhams to help us move from the flooded basement apartment. Brian had been very busy all week, but I felt moved by something much stronger than I could contain to ask of Brian an unusual favor: "Brian, could you meet my family at the Chen's this afternoon?" Brian's response wasn't what I'd expected.

"Did you know that John and I had been prayer partners for the past three years?" That was completely new information for me. I did not have the faintest idea that Brian was a close friend of John's.

"I will be there," Brian assured. Being true to his word, Brian too was waiting when Don and I arrived at the Chen's. Don and I left the Chen's home that evening with a truck full of furniture and a heart overflowing with joy and gratitude. This first meeting would certainly not be the last time we would see the Chen family.

Reminiscently, if we had moved from the Wilson's home two months earlier, it would have been too early, and two months later would've probably been too late. God's timing was perfect! God had appointed a family we never knew or ever heard of to be His special agents. A family we now hold dear in our hearts!

More would be revealed days to come.

The "Secret" Plot

We finally moved into our new apartment. And I liked the way the sunlight forced its way through the trees and crashed upon my bedroom and living room windows, giving an explosive effect of warmth and brightness. One gorgeous spring morning I decided to step outside to inhale the clean, crisp air. My eyes caught something beautiful. I stepped closer toward the thing that had caught my attention.

Aha, just below my window were pretty blooms—vibrant yellow daffodils. The kids got equally excited. They would admire their newfound flower friends first thing every morning. Gorgeous sure is an understatement in attempting to describe the beauty of the daffodils. This was just the beginning of greater discoveries, however. No, there wasn't gold hidden beneath the soil, but to us, finding a fruitful piece of land was like gold. Having spent years in an area where plants failed to grow made my family appreciate this small, fertile plot. Gardening had always been close to my heart, and my Father took that into consideration as well.

Since it was the beginning of spring, it would be a good time to start planting. And what do you know! My doorbell rang. There, standing at the door was Mr. Broderick Morris, a spiritual parent, with a big smile on his face. What did he bring? Pots of healthy-looking plants—tomatoes and zucchini, ready to be planted! Before I asked, the Lord answered. I got my shovel and started digging right away.

The plants burgeoned beyond my imagination. Even tomato seeds from my salad that I'd tossed into the garden grew and produced—abundantly. My desire to plant grew as a seed in God's heart and was transplanted below my window, a simple act of love, with edible results.

I'd begin to learn that each new discovery had become a preamble to an even greater demonstration of love.

One Broken Lid Equals Five Shiny Pots

The courage to believe and do something beyond human reasoning is not always easy. On the journey, I'd taken two pots and a rice cooker. Should I have taken these pots? Did I take them because of a lack of faith?

One evening shortly after I turned on the range burner, I heard "pow!" And then another. *I'm not popping corn, so what could that be?* I pondered. I ran into the kitchen. "Oh, no, not my glass lid," I moaned. I'd turned on the wrong burner. The lid sat helplessly on the range, shattered into pieces.

"Now, what am I going to do?" I whimpered. This was one of my favorite pots that would be coverless. Nevertheless, Don and I sensed that God was up to something—again! So we waited to see how He would replace the broken cover. We prayed. But it took longer than we were patient enough to wait. Fewer pots meant longer time in the kitchen. Realizing I was about to go down a forbidden path—again—I quickly snapped out of rationalizing or letting my reasoning get in the way of another miracle. "I'm sorry, God," I prayed, "I trust you to take care of this one as well. Amen."

Isn't it interesting how, as humans, we tend to forget—so quickly—all the ways the Lord had come through for us in the past? The Creator had worked powerful miracles right before the very eyes of the children of Israel ... and as soon as they encountered a simple obstacle, like getting a drink of water, they grumbled and complained. Oh, how the Lord wants us to trust Him—completely, and let Him weave within each of us the thread of total dependence to strengthen the fabric of the soul.

You see, every journey has roads, and roads have twists and turns. The weather also changes on a journey: It could rain one day, the sun could shine on the next. We cannot rule out the possibility of a storm either. We make rest stops. And at these rest stops, there might be challenges we didn't anticipate—like no water in the restrooms, your sunglasses falling in the toilet, someone smoking in front of you as you make your way to the convenience store—countless things can happen. When these things occur, do you abandon the family trip you've spent months or years planning? Of course not! One never knows what will happen on a journey, and no matter how prepared one is, the inevitable still happens.

A spiritual journey isn't very different. Encountering bumps is all a part of the spiritual experience, which does not mean one should abandon the journey with God. Total dependence on our Guide is of absolute importance. He wants us to be adventurous and spontaneous. Although it would be nice to know all the intricacies of the trip, God does not always reveal what lies ahead. Once we decide to step out with God on a spiritual journey, be prepared for the escapade. We often get impatient because we want to live life our own way or the way to which we are accustomed (I am guilty as charged). Looking back at how God had been leading my own family, I started to feel the warmth of God's sweet assurance trickling down on the inside. I knew it would be all right—He could provide pots, too!

Two days later (after asking God for a few more pots), Don, the kids and I visited some wonderful family friends, the Duncombes, who had invited us to join their family for lunch. Visiting with the Duncombes had always triggered positive reminiscences. And, it was particularly exciting for the kids since they would have a chance to play with their friend Maya, an adorable little girl.

After a great meal, my friend Kemmoree said, "Dee, I know you've just moved ... would you like a few pots? I have a set of five pots that I haven't been using." Did she mention pots? She sure did. What's more, neither Don nor I had discussed a need for pots with our friends. Kemmoree opened her cupboard and handed me not one, not two ... but five shiny, silver pots. Remarkably, one of the pots had a glass lid identical to the one that had been broken, which made a perfect replacement for the coverless pot that happened to be silver, too! With a smile of gratitude, I knew the Lord had done it—again! Does God care about the small details of our hearts? He sure does.

The Bicycle

"Mommy, can I have a bike?" Timmy and Arielle would ask as soon as they saw the kids riding around in our small neighborhood.

"Soon, very soon, the Lord will give you bikes you'll love," I assured them.

"When, Mommy? Why can't He give us bikes now?" Timmy probed, "when is the Lord going to answer our prayers?"

"We don't know, but He will give you bikes," Don and I would remind them.

One beautiful Sunday morning, when the birds seemed at their best and the flowers at their brightest, our family decided to take a casual drive around town in search of garage sales.

"Dear God, please be with us as we go out to look for a bike. Please help us find the bike you have for me. Amen," Timmy prayed earnestly. Not long after we drove out, we stumbled upon a garage sale. We stopped. Don looked around but there weren't any bikes. However, God had a plan. He sent a woman, a total stranger, with a message. The woman, who was also browsing, overheard us talking about getting bikes for the kids.

"Are you looking for a bike?" she asked enthusiastically.

"Yes, we are," Don responded.

"I know where you can get a girl's bike," the stranger exclaimed, and proceeded to give us specific directions to the garage sale she'd happened upon.

"Let's go find that bike!" Don urged.

On our way to finding the garage sale we saw a few other sales and wondered if we should check them out, but Don was convinced that we should keep going, as he sensed that the Lord had given us a specific directive. We kept driving until we arrived at the garage sale to which we had been directed—in a beautiful neighborhood. Right there ... waiting on the lawn was a pretty, pink bike, perfect for a little girl, and great for our budget.

"Hi," a little girl said as she beamed at Timmy and Arielle and whispered something to her daddy. Then her father turned to us, and said, "My daughter says your kids are her friends from Church."

We'd soon learn that this dear family was moving back to California, as they had completed their studies. Everything on their lawn had to go within a few days—they hoped. As for the lady who'd told us about the bike at that particular time and place, who'd also noted she would have bought the bike for her daughter if she didn't already have one, I'd say she was a mystery woman, an angel from above.

But there was no mystery surrounding Arielle's excitement. A permanent smile was affixed to her face. She got her bike at last—her very first bike! She couldn't stop thanking God loudly. Timmy, on the other hand, wasn't a happy camper. He, too, had anticipated getting a bike. But there was only one bike—suitable for a little girl. (His bike was among the items sold in preparation for the trip.)

"But, Mommy, I prayed for a bike for me, not just for Arielle!" he cried. He wailed so hard that afternoon that we worried he would get sick. No word of comfort could give him peace. But what happened next came as a total surprise.

John Chen, God's appointed one, texted me and asked if he could bring a gift over for the kids. *Is it a bike*? I wondered. We all waited anxiously to see how the Lord would answer, because we believed that God would, indeed, provide a bike for Timmy as well.

John finally arrived. He rapped at the front door. He had something red in his hands. A beautiful bike it was, the perfect size for a little boy! Timmy's prayer for a bike of his very own had been answered two days later—a living proof of God's never-ending provision and manifestation of love. There was one problem, however. The bike had no training wheels, and Timmy was not able to balance on his own just yet. But he would, after all, when we made a marvelous discovery!

Approximately three months later, we got another surprise. While the neighbors' kids, along with Timmy and Arielle, were playing in the yard, we noticed that one of the girls' bikes had had its training wheels removed. My husband, Don, had come home a bit early from work that day and had decided to watch the kids play. *The training wheels*, he thought, *perhaps Glenn still has them*. And, just like he thought, Glenn did secure the training wheels. But there was a slight snag: They could not fit Timmy's bike. We contemplated how the training wheels could work, if they could at all. While Don and I tried to figure out a plan, Glenn walked further into his garage. He came back with round objects in his hand.

"Check these out," Glenn said to Don, "I bought these for one of my kids' bikes, but they couldn't fit." Don and Glenn tried the wheels on

Timmy's bike. And what a perfect fit they were! They fit so perfectly that one would think that our neighbor had bought the wheels with Timmy's bike in mind. But he didn't. The training wheels existed long before our son got his bike.

I've learned that God never runs out of ideas or people He can appoint to fulfill His divine purpose(s). God always hears and answers prayers. Sometimes we tend to get impatient when the answer doesn't come right away. But one thing we do know is that God cares enough about each and every need, and He takes each one seriously. We only need to trust Him.

Friends For The Kids

There had been squeaks and screams in the neighborhood. The excitement for my little ones had been mounting to a crescendo. They had been looking forward to having play dates—friends!

Then summer came, and the wheels of busy bikes had started to screech on the hard pavement outside our garage door. Another answer to prayer was on its way. Don and I had prayed long and hard for the right friends for our children, friends who could make positive deposits into their young lives, and they in turn, in theirs. Soon, a few shy contacts would be made, which developed into more exhilarating exchange of laughter between the children whose ages fell between three and seven years old. Later, we had the opportunity to meet their parents, Glenn and Carlene, who had been very affable and kind. Our kids became friends with the Ropers' kids for that summer. For Timmy and Arielle, it was particularly exciting for them since they'd never lived in a neighborhood with small children.

As the friendships grew warm and the kids interacted more frequently, Timmy shared a secret with me. He said, "When I go outside, I use a secret code to let my friends know Arielle and I are out to ride our bikes. I ride my bike up to my friends' apartment and say 'fireworks!'" What great blessing Abigail, Ethan and Gabrielle had brought to our kids! An unforgettable one: Our children's very first summer in the Promised Land.

9.

Wingless Angels

"Surely the Sovereign LORD does nothing without revealing his plan to his servants the prophets" (Amos 3:7, NIV).

"Many of God's appointed angels don't actually have wings; they walk around as our neighbors, friends, and kind strangers."
—*Don Robinson*

A Dream, A Woman, and a Strange Encounter

If you are looking for a place to worship, come to my church," some would say.

"Have you tried that vibrant church over there? I believe you'll like it," another declares with much sincerity. But God had another place—that no one had mentioned—in mind. A place we would not have chosen on our own. Almost everyone we met had discouraged us from choosing the place God would handpick for my family. We listened. We smiled, for we knew too well that our calling didn't fall on the line of comfort and neither could we make a spiritual decision based on the perception of others. "Wherever God wants us to worship, that's where we'll go," we'd respond.

We'd visited different churches in and around the neighborhood, but never felt at home there. One beautiful morning, out of sheer curiosity, Don and I, along with the kids, decided to visit the church we were cautioned not to attend. We knew that what was said was already taking shape, as there was a tinge of apprehension that climbed down my spine as we pulled into the parking lot. You see, that is one of the most damaging parts of any type of gossip—it alters your thinking even before you are given the opportunity to meet or interact with the accused. It's like splashing mud in a tub of clean water.

The service had already started when we arrived. We walked up to the front door. It opened—not automatically, but by a greeter. Her response was not what I'd expected. Shalini sported one of the most dazzling smiles I'd ever received from a greeter. It felt right.

"Are you visiting?" she asked cheerfully.

"Yes," Don responded, "we've just moved here from California."

"Welcome! We are happy to have you worshipping with us today."

"Would you like me to walk with you to the kids' Sabbath school class?"

"Sure, thanks," we responded, almost in unison as we walked briskly, trying to keep up with the greeter's quick, cheerful steps.

When we arrived at the kindergarten room, all eyes turned in our direction—not to scare us, but to welcome us to Sabbath school. There was love everywhere. Although it was a great experience, I was still drawn to the University Church. On the other hand, our children had fallen in love with their new-found Sabbath school and would cry whenever Don or I mentioned visiting another church.

"God, is this the church you have selected for us?" we prayed. We waited for the familiar voice. It responded. The voice affirmed. The Lord had made us stewards over many talents and spiritual gifts that we wanted to use for His glory. We knew that if the Lord wanted us to serve in a specific way, He would arrange His appointments—and He would make it known to us, without coercion.

The following week we went back to the church for another microscopic look. Our experience? Even better than when we first visited. It felt homely and we knew, deep inside that, this was the place God had chosen, contrary to the many voices. Then we got a letter in the mail. A welcome letter it was. That sealed it. Village would be our place of worship! God was leading and we were not going to go against Him. He had a plan that He would reveal when our hearts were ready...

Another person we met on our first visit to Village was a sweet lady named Anna Chiarenza, who happened to be substituting for Lori Bahlmann, a kindergarten Sabbath school teacher. As if divinely designed, our kids walked over to Anna's desk and sat in the tiny chairs arranged at the round, wooden table. Anna smiled. We felt attracted to her Christ-like personality. After Sabbath school, the kids talked about their class and their new teacher, Anna. But Anna wouldn't be there the next week to greet them, as she was only filling in for Lori.

Seeing and feeling all the love, my family accepted Anna's invitation to go to the church's potluck after the worship service. We felt at home since the one face we could remember was already there serving with love. One of the things that made our fellowship so special during lunch was that Anna cared to remember my kids' names and greeted them personally as they approached her table. I took to her too ... and soon discovered we had something in common: We had a passion to work for God!

Anna and I talked. I shared a little about my journey with her, and she shared a bit about hers with me. During this exchange, I learned that her husband, as well as her dad, had recently passed away. The freshness of the loss was evident as the tears dampen her eyes. *How could she smile so warmly with such pain lingering in her heart*? I wondered. Then the answer came bouncing in my thoughts: *It's the love of Jesus. Her passion to serve the way Christ did.* That love radiated and animated her whole being. Anna's two beautiful girls, Maria and Susannah, sported similar smiles that warmed my heart. I believe God had chosen Anna to confirm His decision for the church we should attend. I needed to meet her. Anna's eyes conveyed Christ's love. Her eyes unbolted the window of her soul and the door to her church.

God Isn't Done With Me Yet

I'd been searching for Christians who really love not just with their hearts but with their eyes as well. There is something about the eyes that when Christ is seen through them, you experience redemption, acceptance. I needed to have that encounter. In my heart, I'd planned to walk away from the church and never look back! I felt I'd had it—enough bickering, enough criticism, enough judging, enough—! Growing up in the church, I had encountered believers who seemed to think that they had some kind of special connection with heaven that other Christians didn't have, and, therefore, it would be their responsibility to tell you where, when, why and how to serve God. These persons I would call "Self-appointed Administrative Assistants to the Throne of God."

"The music is from hell," says one.

"Look at that boy singing with his hands in his pockets," declares another.

"That hairstyle couldn't be Christ-like," someone else asserts.

"Don't sit with your legs crossed in church; it's irreverent," says yet another, while in their own lives incongruities were evident.

The Lord wants each of us to come to him with zits, freckles ... and warts, and submit to the power of His Holy Spirit, which is available to every man and every woman, every boy and every girl. God is an amazing

God. He loves us all. And God's ultimate desire is to woo us—not to whip us into submission—into a love relationship with Him, where each person can embrace the opportunity to understand His heart of grace. The closer we get to God, the better our relationship will be with each other as brothers and sisters.

Today, there seems to be an unpleasant breath that forms an ominous cloud on the neck of the youth, stifling the growth of tomorrow's leaders. I didn't think I needed to go to church to be spiritually poisoned. My heart felt broken into a million pieces, ten times over. I'd wanted nothing to do with the church again. Having made this decision several months before relocating, the Lord reminded me as my family traveled across country that, He would not let me go without a fight. He whispered in my ear, "You are precious to Me."

Who gave you all those talents and spiritual gifts? What do you plan to do with them? How about My little children? They need you to be their spiritual guide. I wrestled with the Lord through bitter tears. I was adamant, and so was my Father. He would not let me go. And during our cross-country trip, something amazing happened.

Like Saul I met the Lord, not stricken with blindness, but with overwhelming demonstrations of pure Agape love. God comforted me like a parent cradling a hurting child. He opened my eyes to His plan for me in ways He hadn't ever before. He wiped away the dross of discouragement. He infused my heart with hope. He gave me a complete makeover. He gave me a different me—the *me* I'd always desired to be. As God sent Ananias to see Saul, so was Anna led to me. Anna was my Ananias! How interesting that these two names are somewhat similar. As I thought about this divine appointment, something even more interesting resurfaced in my mind—the dream!

The dream I'd mentioned in an earlier chapter was now taking shape. It came alive. The comfort I'd extended in my first dream on my *first* night in Michigan had come to life in the church's fellowship hall (cafeteria) during lunch, my *first* visit to Anna's church. Was it ordained that Anna and I would offer words of comfort to each other on this *first* encounter? In one of my conversations with Anna she expressed something prophetic. This, she mentioned not knowing the story behind the story. She said: "The Lord has brought your family to Village for a purpose. You are here to make a difference."

I'll allow the rest of the story to unfold in God's perfect timing...

Captions Of Our Journey

Our Taiwanese students with Don and me in Kaohsiung, Taiwan.

The final meal on our "box table" before the journey

Journey sandals

Missouri (the only state we didn't do a layover).

The 4 × 8 U-Haul trailer that transported
our belongings is attached to our
SUV.

Timmy and Arielle, little missionaries, at the Islas' home in Sunrise, Arizona. Our first stopover.

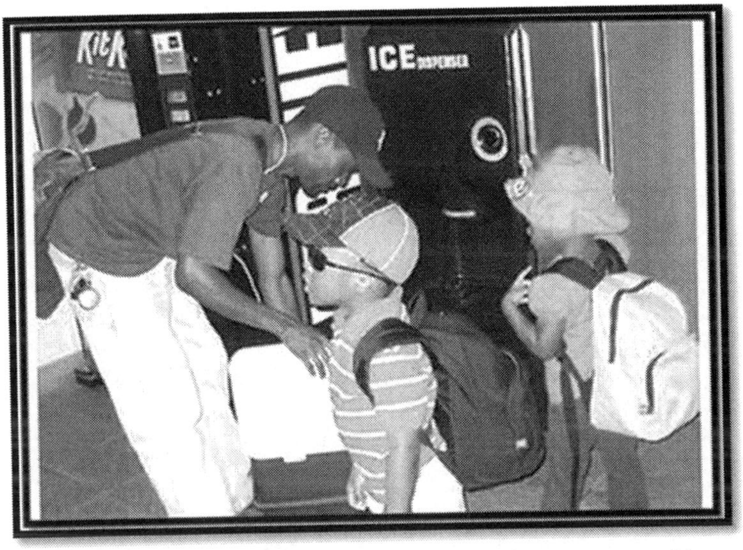

Don and the kids filling up our cooler with ice at a motel in Albuquerque, New Mexico.

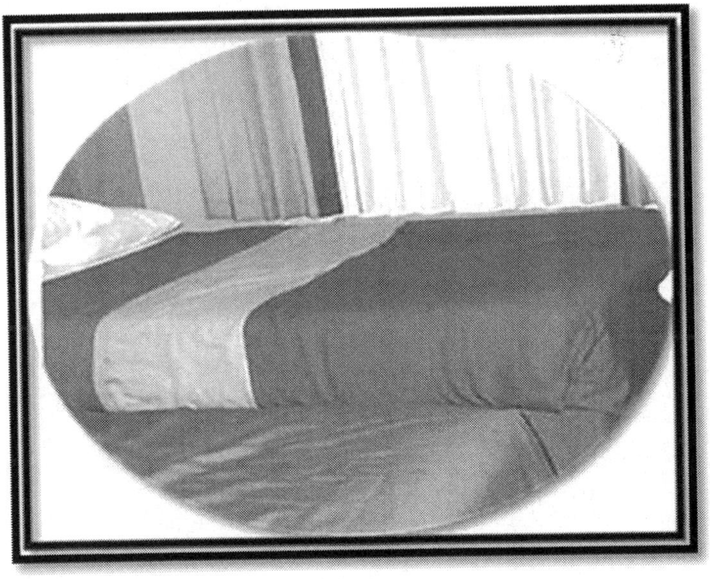

Oklahoma! The room in which we learned where we would go!

Me with my wonderful husband, Don—my faithful partner in ministry.

10.

Peculiar Interventions

Faith Snacks!

"For I am the LORD your God who takes hold of your right hand and says to you, Do not fear; I will help you" (Isaiah 41:13, NIV).

- "Blessed are those who worship the God of heaven."
  – *Arielle Robinson; 5 years old*
- "The blood of Jesus Christ is to save you, not to harm you."
  – *Timothy Robinson; 6 years old*
- "Adversity can be a dreaded foe or a great flight instructor—it either clips our wings or teaches us how to soar above our circumstances."
  – *Don Robinson*

A Stranger's Offer

By Don Robinson

The lights on the dashboard suddenly grew dim. *That's odd.* I thought to myself as I tried to figure out what was going on. The radio went silent and without even a slight cough, the engine died! It was less than thirty minutes earlier that I'd e-mailed my wife, Dionne, telling her I was leaving work soon. Now there I was, stranded—with a dead truck in the sweltering summer heat.

As I walked toward what I thought was a repair shop, an SUV pulled up beside me. "Hello, do you need some help," a kind man asked. Sitting beside him was his lovely wife who smiled gracefully as if to say, *It's okay.*

I briefly mentioned my predicament and asked to be excused as I returned to a call I was on with my insurance company. "They are sending a tow truck to take my van to a nearby shop," I said to the curious stranger. The couple, Joe and Roberta, invited me to sit in their air-conditioned SUV while I waited for the tow truck. There was a strange sense of peace and security that reminded me that Someone loving was watching over me. My new friends entertained me for more than one hour and helped me create an action plan while we waited. The cool air from their truck and the love from their hearts provided a refreshing respite that starkly contrasted the torrid temperature, with humidity above eighty percent on the outside.

Joe and Roberta shared that they had had a similar experience in Chicago two weeks earlier, only that time they were the ones being helped. I was further moved when I realized that they were actually on their way to a restaurant to eat dinner. But when they saw my vehicle by the side of the road, they opted to help and delayed their evening meal.

Finally the tow truck came, picked up my disabled vehicle and brought it to a repair shop in town. My new friends helped me retrieve some of my stuff from my car, then gave me a ride home. Their interest and concern drove questions across the paths of my mind. "Who are these people?" "Why are they so kind to me—a stranger?" Parking the queries—temporarily, I thanked them profusely for their kindness and waved goodbye, not knowing if we'd ever meet again.

As their car drove up to the end of the road and disappeared behind the apartment complexes that lined the street, the strange encounter, the thrill of being helped by total strangers enveloped me. My family listened in awe as I related what had transpired. I had no idea who those wonderful people were, but what I do know was that they were God-sent! What happened next, however, had totally caught me off guard.

The next day while I was at work I noticed a missed call from Joe, as we'd exchanged numbers while we awaited the arrival of the tow truck. I listened to the message. Then, returned the call as soon as I could. "Hello?" Joe said, "how's it going? I just wanted you to know that I am more than willing to cover the expenses for your truck."

I stuttered a bit, "Um, thanks, but I'll be all right."

Joe continued, "If you'd like to make payments back to me in small increments that would be fine, too."

"Hmm, I don't usually do that ... but thanks for your thoughtfulness."

But Joe insisted on helping me as though a divine force in the unseen world were in control of every word he spoke. Finally, I accepted—after feeling inner peace ...

A stranger is offering to pay for my car repairs? That's odd, I thought. I walked back to my desk, flooded with the feeling of a divine presence. "This has got to be God at work." I muttered to myself, trying not to look like a crazy man talking to himself.

God does use unconventional ways to fulfill His purpose(s). And this was one of them. God had sent comfort and reassurance at a time when I needed it most! No matter what situation you may find yourself in, God is there. He is faithful to His promise—"He will not leave us nor forsake us." Whatever it takes to bring us relief, He will do!

A Dis-Appointment That Turned Into a Re-Appointment

Don Robinson

One early Wednesday morning I made my way to work all ready to teach two students I had scheduled for that class. Upon my arrival, at approximately six o'clock, I noticed that the students had dropped the class. *It had to be sometime between the previous evening and early in the morning,* I thought, *because when I checked my roster before leaving work, the names were still there.*

I went to the classroom, anyway. While I was there, I noticed someone approaching the room. It was a gentleman whose name was not on the schedule, but he wanted to know if it was OK to take the class. This man, however, had much on his heart to reveal. The class took on a different flavor. He mentioned that he'd grown up in a Christian home, but had walked away. As it turned out, he was a prodigal searching for the way back home. The more the gentleman shared, the greater the joy that spread all over his bearded face.

After an exciting lesson, he started recounting Bible stories, including Jacob's fearful anticipation of Esau, even after so many years. I seized the opportunity to invite him to take the journey home, since the Father was not mad at him. We prayed together. He left leaping like a calf released from a stall.

God had simply made room for a divine appointment that morning. What a God!

The Mozart CD

Approximately five years ago we purchased a package of classical CDs for our young children. Our son, Timmy, loved listening to the different classical pieces and would even name the composer from just listening to a short presentation.

But, accidentally, the CD broke, the Mozart CD. Timmy was disappointed. I was, too. Regrettably, we put away the broken CD—and forgot about it.

Then one day, John came by with a large, brown box. I opened it eagerly. I spotted something familiar. Inside the box, stashed neatly in a corner, was a little case that enclosed a CD—a Mozart CD!

Even in this small situation, God showed up. He did not send other CDs we'd already have—but the very replacement needed!

Even before we ask, the Lord promises, He will answer.

The One-Dollar Coat

I'd been looking for a winter coat since the time we arrived in Michigan. Everyone had a story to tell about the abrasive winters there. "Are you ready for it?" friends (and strangers) would ask. The price for a really good winter coat was astronomical, and who could afford that? Certainly not us. We had just moved and Don was still waiting to pick up a job.

One sunny Sunday morning, just about the beginning of fall when the leaves had started to turn, my family decided to drive over to Indiana, where we would browse around in the stores there to find an affordable coat. We'd heard that prices there were inexpensive. But on our way, a huge garage sale caught our attention. We stopped. And, what do you know! There was a winter coat. The cost? One dollar! We loved it. The color and style suited me well ... and it was in great condition.

Do any of our concerns escape His eye? No, not one of His children's needs escapes the Father's loving eye!

11.

Mysterious Ways

"And this same God who takes care of me will supply all your needs from his glorious riches, which have been given to us in Christ Jesus" (Philippians 4:19, NLT).

"Life is a collection of many moments: make each one count. And while you're at it, don't forget the people around you, for they are little gems that line your path."
–Don Robinson

A Peculiar Impression

What a strange day it was! It was such an odd day that I literally trembled with emotions that fluctuated between anger, fear and frustration. Even more anomalous, I was impressed to turn on the television, something that had not been a part of my routine for years. But on this day, I felt pushed to turn on the TV. At first I stopped at a cartoon channel that seemed interesting. I paused for a moment and then kept on surfing. This time I knew I was at the right channel (a talk show), where the host had been discussing a topic that arrested my attention—*Living Well.* During the show the host demonstrated—using a special type of blender—how to mix various types of fruit and vegetable smoothies. The exact type of smoothies I'd enjoyed at the Coleman's.

Something about this show made it even more interesting. You see, my husband and I had planned to procure a similar type of mixer, so I became intrigued and felt that the Lord was affirming this desire. What's more, the powerful blender was on special. Calling in to order it would land us a discount, which seemed like a good investment. "I've got to tell Don about this," I said softly as I picked up the phone. Don liked the idea and promised to give it a try.

"I'll give them a call and let you know," Don said. Moments later the phone rang ... and I wondered how he'd made the call so quickly. My gut gave me that something-is-wrong type of signal.

"Hon, I've just had the strangest experience," Don said, "I can't find my wallet." The wallet was gone, which made it impossible for him to make the payment over the phone. I could not believe my ears. Don looked everywhere, made a few phone calls, but no one had seen his wallet that contained "his life!" The one place that he did not contact was closed and would not be opened until the next day. He'd gone to the post office earlier that day. We checked our accounts, and there were no suspicious activities of any kind.

Morning broke. Don contacted the one place he hadn't yet telephoned. "We found your wallet, and it is here at the post office," a clerk said. What a relief! Don had been going all day not knowing his wallet was missing—until I was led to watch that program, something I hadn't done in years. And, seeing the blender we both wanted, stirred in me a desire to contact Don, which led to the discovery of the missing wallet. What a God!

We thought his life was wrapped up in the contents of his wallet, but the Lord wanted to remind us that our life is in His hand! Nothing in this world is more important than feeling secure in one's relationship with God. When all the earthly possessions we own are lost, we can find ourselves in Jesus Christ. Are you holding on to something you think is indispensable? Let your Maker take care of it for you.

The Mysterious Wasp Escape

It had been pretty hot and humid. The clouds gathered slowly as though a procession for a dignitary were in progress. On that summer day, the children and I decided to go to the library for a presentation on owls. Since we'd planned to walk there, and not wanting to be late, I decided to get everything done as quickly as possible. But as fate would have it, I rushed into the kids' room only to be greeted by a flying creature—a wasp, the biggest I'd ever seen! I gasped, trying hard not to convey any feeling of fright to startle the kids. They noticed anyway. "Is it the same wasp that came into our room yesterday, Mommy?" Timmy asked.

"Looks like it," I said.

I prayed and believed that the Lord would deliver the wasp into my hands as He'd handed over Goliath into David's hands. I held my own "sling" in hand. "Lord, you are much more powerful than a little insect, so please lead it through that open window," I prayed, feeling terrified of the big wasp. But the wasp did not budge. *It's getting late,* I thought, *and I needed to get the kids dressed, but we are all scared ... ugh. I wish Don were here to help,* I moaned. The fractious wasp flew to another window in the room, attempting to squeeze through the window screen, but its body was more than twice the size of the ventilation holes in the screen. I kept on praying.

Where is it? I wondered. *I hope it's not on my head or on my shoulder,* I thought. I edged closer to the window, fearing it would reappear and startle me, but the wasp was not there. Since my eyes were fixed on its every move (and since it was pretty big), I knew it didn't move from its window location—or did it?

Through an open window? Yes. Through the screen? Not possible, I reasoned. But the Lord did the unexpected: He led the wasp through a closed window screen with holes much too small for a big wasp to crawl through—mysteriously! Sometimes we pray for the Lord to resolve our situations a certain way, to lead us through doors that we ourselves have opened. But, the Lord has more than a million ways to answer our prayers. Let God lead—even if what He is doing doesn't add up in our own eyes. Why? He knows best. And just like He did for the wasp, He'll do for you: make a way through a seemingly impossible path!

God's Two Hundred Dollars

By Don Robinson

It was another beautiful service. Pastor Larry had preached his heart out, and the spirit of God filled the building. At the end of the service, as is customary, we'd shake the pastor's hand at the door and share how blessed we had been as a result of his stirring sermon. This Sabbath, however, before exiting the church, I noticed a brother sitting in the pew—alone. I walked over to where he was sitting and greeted him. He greeted me back with a smile. We talked for a while.

During our conversation, I learned that this brother was having tremendous challenges—discouraging ones. His most eminent need was that he needed two hundred dollars to pay his electric bill. If this bill wasn't paid within a few days, he and his family would be forced to live in the dark—without electricity to keep the house warm or power to preserve his food in the refrigerator. He did not have the money.

When my family and I got home that day, I shared what I'd learned about our hurting brother. We prayed. How much did he need to pay the bill? All the cash we had in hand! At this moment, faith and flesh began a fierce battle. Two hundred dollars was all we had as extra cash! This sum we had received from a previous landlord who'd owed us money from our deposit (as mentioned in chapter six). For a while I did not remember this treasure, until one day, it suddenly dawned on me. Now, someone needed all the money I'd just received. *My family needs it, too,* I contemplated. Dionne and I prayed and believed that God would provide for our brother, but probably not through us.

Several hours had passed and although I didn't discuss it further, there was a nagging, lingering feeling that the Lord wanted me to move beyond the flesh. My family needed the money, but my brother had a more imminent need. *To have one's electricity disconnected during the winter sure isn't fun. It could be me,* I thought.

Then at around sunset, the issue was brought back to the table: *Call Ben* to see how he and his wife are doing,* the Spirit prompted as my wife and I settled in bed, ready to retire for the night. It was already 10 o'clock; all cell phones had been turned off, with no plans to talk to anyone on the outside. But I just couldn't switch off the light that kept flashing in my mind. This light made Ben's face increasingly visible, leaving an aurora.

The revelation of Ben's plight was especially chilling to me when I considered that the end of the cold season was still several weeks or even months away. *What if God wanted me to pay the bill for Ben?* I thought. My family had set the money aside for a special project. We had just moved into a new apartment and needed a washing machine as well as beds for our two kids. It is important to note that it wasn't Ben who approached me; I obeyed a compelling urge to stop by and talk to him and that's how I got to learn of his plight.

That Monday night I followed my wife's suggestion, which was really the audible expression of a deafening inner voice, and telephoned Ben.

"Hello?" Ben said.

"How is it going?" I asked, hoping that his situation was fixed. However, Ben related that he was still not out of the dark, but that the electric company had given him an extension until the Thursday of that week.

"I have some money that my family had been saving to purchase a washing machine and a bunk bed for our kids," I revealed, "but we could give you this money to pay your electric bill. And you don't have to worry about paying it back." What Ben said next was electrifying.

"We have a washing machine here that we've never really used. We can give it to you ... and I can build a bunk bed for your kids," Ben said excitedly as he thanked me profusely for the generosity shown to him.

We marveled at God's goodness. God had met my family's needs when we made the sacrifice to meet someone else's need. We've shared this testimony not to pat ourselves on our shoulders, but to amplify God's graciousness and faithfulness.

The next day I gave Ben all the cash we had—$200, and picked up an almost-brand-new washing machine. He even came by our apartment to help install it, bringing along the two (exact) hoses that would be needed for hot and cold water.

This experience has brought to mind the story of Abraham who was willing to give up his only son, Isaac, in obedience to God's will. Another story also came to mind: The woman who gave all she had—out of her poverty. "Calling His disciples to Him, Jesus said, 'Truly I tell you, this poor widow has put more into the treasury than all the others. They all gave out of their wealth; but she, out of her poverty, put in everything—all she had to live on'" (Mark 12:43-44).

When God calls us to do something that seems impossible or unrealistic, we should not shrink back, for He always has a better plan—one that will not cause pain but bring abundant joy.

Although we greatly appreciated Ben's offer to build us a bunk bed, we didn't want him to divert his time and attention on something that would not bring him much-needed income. We continued praying and looking around for a bunk bed. During this period, we gave our kids the opportunity to use our bed, while my wife and I used sleeping bags. It was a wonderful adventure that had brought us even closer as a family, and had given us a clearer sense of our priorities. We shared with the kids what the Lord had wanted us to do with the money we'd been saving for their bunk bed ... and they, too, joined in giving God praise for what He would do next.

*Name has been changed

Bunk Beds?

That same week, our neighbors who'd lived next door on the same building, told us they were moving to California, and that they would be having a garage sale. We asked if they had a bunk bed for sale. They didn't. But, interestingly, they indicated that they did have two double beds, complete with mattresses, box springs and covers—all in excellent condition. The cost? A price too ridiculous to mention. We purchased the beds.

Our loving Lord took care of the kids' beds ... and the washer—perfectly, without the two hundred dollars we'd wanted to preserve self-interestedly! Oh, what God can do when we trust Him completely! God did not have bunk beds in mind. That was our idea He overruled. He gave us twin beds.

Sometimes, we tend to come up with our own ideas, thinking that if it is a good idea, it must be God's idea.

Is God calling you, my friend, to be more sensitive to the needs of others? To be more empathetic and altruistic toward someone—who could be right under your nose?

When God invites us to join Him, may our answer be, "Here I am, Lord, use me."

100 Degrees Fahrenheit and No Air

Our new apartment had no air conditioner! This, however, did not spark concern since we'd been told that an air conditioner wouldn't be necessary in the summer. But things would change drastically after we arrived.

Winters that were usually harsh, had melted into mere fall-like temperatures. By summer, a drought hit the region. What a calamity! Farmers stood helplessly, with jaws dropped as they watched their crops wilt and die. The "fruit basket of America" would be empty. We'd planned to go fruit picking that summer, but that would not be—large strawberries had been reduced to mere pebble-size berries.

Looking back at the intriguing Bible story about a man named Abraham, whom God had called to go to a place that Abraham knew nothing about, I can see some similarities between his story and my own story.

Note, Abraham did not know his destination, but he obeyed. Now, look at what happened after Abraham arrived at the place God had handpicked for him: "...There was a famine in the land, and Abram went down to Egypt to live there for a while because the famine was severe" (Genesis 12:10).

You see, when God calls His children to follow Him, life will not always be easy. In fact, it seems to get worse before it gets better. There will be disappointments, tragedies and all kinds of setbacks. But we have to learn to trust in God and not in our circumstances. No matter what our conditions might be, as long as God is there, we are safe. This assurance my family would come to embrace when the trials burned at the core of what we held dear. We had to hold strong to our faith when our motivation became parched, when we ached for a downpour of His promised blessing.

With the midday heat rising to as high as 102 degrees Fahrenheit, so was the wave of discouragement. Like the Children of Israel, the temptation was there to look back, to long for what we'd left behind. But God, in His mercy, sent a reprieve through a small window fan Don had bought and four standing fans we'd gotten from the Wilsons. What a relief! We never thought the day would come when we would be in a house that was over 100 degrees—without air! As we followed the news and learned how the heat had been affecting people, especially the elderly and children, we became concerned. Our two young children, four and five years old, sweated like pigs. Seeking to find relief, we discovered that things were becoming even more discouraging.

Our only bathtub started filling up with dirty water that wouldn't drain. We notified the property manager. "Sorry ... I will get the plumber to come over ... tomorrow," the owner said.

"Do you have someone whom you could call in case of an emergency?" I asked.

"I'm sorry, but I do not..." the property manager responded. This sure was a real test of patience. Hot, sweaty, and can't shower?! Dark clouds of discouragement drifted in and gave way to a hail of tears. Nevertheless, we kept on trusting. The clouds parted and a ray of hope peeked through our throbbing hearts.

The Lord heard our call and helped my dear husband figure out a way to fix the tub. The water disappeared with a big gargle, as though it had just disinfected the tub. We were finally able to shower and enjoy temporary relief. Thanking God for the little things we enjoy every day—effortlessly—should be a part of our daily lives, as we won't notice their significance, until they are taken away.

For the remaining days of the heat wave, it was like God had sent a special invisible canopy that hung mysteriously over our home to keep us cool. The house felt comfortable—as if an air conditioning unit were running. We were amazed at God's goodness toward us. Despite the torrid heat and high humidity, no one in the family got sick or picked up a heat rash. Why? God had sent special air from heaven! And, did I tell you that the kids slept like logs all through the night—despite the heat?!

God's Promises Never Fail

Reflection and Recommitment

Throughout this journey I've often found myself whispering: "This doesn't make sense." But who says it has to make sense to us? I've learned that trusting God is a much better option than a slew of information. Is trusting easy? Not at all. As humans we like to know, don't we? I do. I like to know how things are going to unfold—step by step. But God uprooted that, as it was getting in the way of our relationship. He took me on a date blindfolded—the first step in moving me away from my natural inclinations. God required total trust. He wanted me to learn how to depend on Him.

Sometimes you and I might lose confidence in God's way, thinking that we have a better plan, a more user-friendly idea, especially when we sense that God isn't working according to our schedule. The tendency is to rush ahead of Him and take things into our own hands. When we do, the most likely result is failure, a sticky situation in which we'd rather not get trapped.

When God gives His children any kind of revelation, it does not always mean that everything will be unfolded in a day or two. Sometimes it takes years. Just like the Bird of Paradise flower that blooms five long years after it has been planted.

Dear friend, God has a beautiful plan for your life. Others may sometimes question your walk of obedience with God and may cast shadows of doubt along your path. But you will have to choose whose voice you will obey. Someone who was not present when God was speaking to you has no authority to speak of or against your journey with your Savior. Stay close to God's Word and His wonderful promises, for in then you will find comfort, guidance and hope.

God calls people who are willing to go with Him, not perfect people. God has always chosen to use erring human beings who are frail and prone to making all kinds of mistakes—something only God does; He meets us right where we are and takes us where we ought to be. His thoughts are not like ours and neither are our ways like His. This brings comfort to followers of God, just knowing that God forgives, forgets and continues to equip His erring children.

With this assurance, Don and I have committed ourselves, our whole life to the God Who has kept us on His path since the day we met—since the day he and I knelt on the university green to ask God if it was His desire for us to be together.

My God has been there with us through some of the most discouraging times of our life—the times when we'd rather give up than follow through with His assignments. But in those times, there had always been a voice, an encouraging voice, saying, "Stay on the path with Me; I love you." I know it was the voice of God. And, our God has been there with us in some of our most exciting moments: those delightful occasions when we celebrated the births of our beloved children, who've brought so much joy, so much life, so much purpose to Don's and my life.

We are aware that the Lord has great plans for us as a family. And, throughout this journey, we have committed ourselves to doing His will, as we seek to be a blessing to everyone we meet.

What has God been calling you to do? Are you feeling weary of the journey on which the Lord is taking you? Do you sometimes feel like you want to take over because you have a better idea? Do you think that what God has called you to do is impossible? The road may be long and dreary, but remember God never fails.

Dionne Robinson

Epilogue

The Journey in Retrospect

Don Robinson:

Up to a year before we set out on our pilgrim journey from California to Michigan, I'd never imagined myself living anyplace where I'd have to wear snow gear for more than a few days in a row. Living in sunny Southern California we could travel to the mountains to enjoy the snow, go to the beach for a splash, and get back home to make dinner—all in one day. Despite the convenient living, there was a lingering sense that the Lord wanted me to break through the limits of my own thinking.

The desire to relocate was becoming increasingly stronger, but boundaries of where I would call my home had been clearly marked off in my mind. That was until one day, standing in my kitchen, I heard myself say to my wife, Dionne, "A person's world changes instantly in his mind." The reality of what I'd said sent shock waves down my spine and I burst out laughing, knowing full well what was going to happen.

Suffice it to say that those months leading up to our exodus from California were among the most trying, and yet, most spiritually transforming. I had such peace about our future that when it came time to turn in my resignation for my teaching job, I signed and submitted that letter as though it were a job-acceptance letter. Yet, during the waiting period, our patience was severely tried and our faith tested in the fires of perseverance. We had a strong conviction that our Land of Promise was Michigan—a state that carried one of the highest unemployment rates in the country. Or was it Maryland? Maryland had suddenly shown promise, just days before our departure from California. We'd sent out what seemed like hundreds of job applications and received no hopeful response. In the end we were compelled to set out on that epic journey into the unknown, guided by a faith in the same God who'd called Abram to leave his homeland for "a land which I will show you."

Through the preparation period, the seven-day journey to Michigan, and our early experiences in the Promised Land, we learned to develop a deeply personal relationship with God. Whether it was through taking us hundreds of miles on failing brakes, finding a place to call home, or securing the perfect job, it was obvious that our lives were being guided by a force that was much greater than luck, and more calculated than mere coincidence—this force was God! And our lives would never again be the same!

Acknowledgements

A note of gratitude cannot be overlooked, especially when significant contributions have been deposited into the life of another. With this in mind, there wouldn't be enough space in this book to thank all the people who've made such deposits in Don's and my life—in some big or small way. This book is a reflection of all the positive impact others have made on our life, and, particularly, the contributions made to this leg of our journey into the unknown with our God! All the small ripples of kindness and support have created an ocean of possibilities, making this book a success.

All thanks, glory and honor to our heavenly Father, our Supreme Guide, who surrounds us with His favor and love. He has placed numerous testimonies upon our hearts to bring blessing and hope, not only to my family, but also to everyone who reads this book.

Words fail to express how grateful we are for our wonderful parents: Neil & Zoebel Wilson and Ransford & Lucille Robinson. Without them, we would not be here to tell a single story. They gave us the greatest gift ever—life!

Thanks to Dr. David Dudley and Dr. Martin Hanna for giving us empathetic ears when we needed someone to listen.

Thanks to Peter & Lorelei Cress, Mark & Leslie von Esch, and Stuart & Karen Tyner for their words of comfort, kindness, love and hospitality.

A huge thank-you to Pastor Julio Tabuenca for the indisputable role he has played—even when this journey was yet a seed in the heart of God.

Heartfelt gratitude to the El Centro English, El Centro Spanish, and Brawley Seventh-day Adventist churches for giving us the opportunity to serve in so many different ways.

A special note of thanks to Irasema Ramirez—one of the most caring persons we've ever met—for her love, kindness and thoughtfulness.

A big thank-you to Roger & Judy Morse, Mar & Liza, and Lorena Grijalva for the kindness they've shown and all the help they've extended, especially in the days before leaving for this special journey.

Thanks to all our friends and family who texted us throughout the entire trip to make sure we were doing okay.

A very big thank-you to Jesús & Susanna Garcia for their sincerity, thoughtfulness and Christ-like love they've shown to us.

Thanks to Lydia & Henry Dodge, Linda Heater and Andy Erickson for making positive deposits into our life.

Sincere appreciation to Susan Smith, Marvin & Joan Pinder, Don Dudley, Pastor Gerald Penick, and all those at Southeastern California Conference who believed in us and created opportunities for us to grow and be involved in various types of ministries.

A note of gratitude to the Islas family for welcoming us into their beautiful home on the first major stop of our journey of faith.

Thanks to all my brothers and sisters, nieces and nephews for their unfailing support, respect and kindness.

Heartfelt thanks to Brian Manley, Larry & Brenda Woodhams, John & DeEtta Chen, Vincent & Kemmoree Duncombe, Terry & Helen Hayes, Juliet & Jerry Horton, Stacey-Ann Nicely, Glenn & Carlene Roper, and Pastor Larry & Kathie Lichtenwalter for the unique God-appointed roles they've played on our journey.

Special thanks to Vicki & Mark Cudanin for being the first to invite us home for a delectable Sabbath lunch as we shopped around for a church to call home. Their kind gesture stays in our hearts.

Thanks to Betty Guy and Elizabeth Burrows for the important roles they've played in a fundamental chapter on this amazing journey.

How could I close a page of thanksgiving without expressing deep gratitude to my loving and dear partner in ministry, best friend, wonderful father of my children, and an incredible husband to me—Don! Thanks for serving God faithfully with me, hand in hand, and for being the wind under my wings. His loving words of encouragement, warm sense of humor, devotion, Christ-like demeanor, and support have made my life complete!

And to my beautiful children: Mommy loves you dearly!

About The Author

Dionne Robinson is the founder of WalkInFaith Books. She is the author of *Experiencing God in Everyday Ordinary Things* and inspirational writer at *From The Heart Inspirational Picture Quotes.* Dionne Robinson holds a Master of Arts degree in curriculum and instruction from La Sierra University, a Bachelor of Science degree in counseling psychology from Northern Caribbean University, and a certificate in teaching English as a foreign language from the University of California, Riverside. She is the last of eight children, and the first to obtain a master's degree.

Dionne and her husband, Don, served as missionaries in Taiwan, where they taught English and Bible. Mrs. Robinson is a certified teacher who has taught English and reading at the junior-high level at Calexico Mission School, California.

At her local church (before relocating to the Midwest), Dionne was elected to serve as one of the first female elders on a male-dominated team. In addition to being an elder, she has served as assistant family life director, special programs coordinator, and in various other capacities in which she has worked faithfully. As a motivational speaker and writer, Dionne Robinson has been impacting lives positively in ways that are unique to her special calling.

Presently, Mrs. Robinson is homeschooling her two first graders while finding fun and creative ways to develop her writing projects and expand her publishing enterprise. Dionne and Don are very much in love and look forward to growing old together.

Faithful Partners in Ministry

Don Robinson holds a Master of Arts degree in religion, with an emphasis in school psychology. He has also earned a Bachelor of Arts degree in religion and an Associate of Science degree in business administration. Mr. Robinson is a certified teacher, who has taught religion and mathematics for a number of years at Calexico Mission School, to senior high school and middle school students. Simultaneously, he has served as the academy's guidance counselor.

Don is an ordained elder, who has also served as family life director, youth leader, worship leader, interim pastor, and in many other offices within his religious organization. As an inspirational speaker and life coach, Don has touched many lives in positive, meaningful ways.

Don Robinson is the last of eight children, and the first to acquire a master's degree. He is happily married to his college sweetheart, Dionne, and has been enjoying his two energetic children.

Timmy is a deep thinker. He likes to analyze and synthesize concepts, regardless of their complexity. At five years old, Timmy enthusiastically started writing his first children's book that he hopes to get published soon. He is an avid reader who enjoys reading interesting books.

In addition to reading, Timmy likes to write, learn about nature, tell stories, entertain, sing, dramatize Bible stories, ride his bike, and play with friends. His favorite subjects are math, English, music and science. He also enjoys participating in swimming and gymnastics. Without Timmy's contribution, this book would not be possible.

Arielle is a precocious little girl who started reading on the fourth-grade level at three years old. She is excited about her children's book that she hopes to get published soon. In addition to reading, Arielle enjoys writing, singing, laughing, sharing, storytelling, dramatizing Bible stories, and playing with friends. Her favorite subjects are English, music, math ... and social studies. She also enjoys swimming and gymnastics. Arielle's contribution has made the completion of this book possible.

"My people will live in safety, quietly at home. They will be at rest" (Isaiah 32:18, NLT).

"Hope says: It shall be well.
Faith assures: It's possible.
Patience implores: Be still."
– *Dionne Robinson*

50786215R00086

Made in the USA
Charleston, SC
07 January 2016